Black Baseball
in New York City

ALSO BY LARRY LESTER

Baseball's First Colored World Series:
The 1924 Meeting of the Hilldale Giants
and Kansas City Monarchs
(McFarland, 2006; softcover 2014)

Rube Foster in His Time: On the Field
and in the Papers with Black Baseball's
Greatest Visionary (McFarland, 2012)

Black Baseball in New York City

An Illustrated History, 1885–1959

LARRY LESTER

McFarland & Company, Inc., Publishers
Jefferson, North Carolina

Except where otherwise credited,
all photographs are courtesy NoirTech Research.

ISBN (print) 978-1-4766-7046-1 ∞
ISBN (ebook) 978-1-4766-2941-4

LIBRARY OF CONGRESS CATALOGUING DATA ARE AVAILABLE

BRITISH LIBRARY CATALOGUING DATA ARE AVAILABLE

Front cover: (clockwise, from top left) 1911 Lincoln Giants,
Leroy "Satchel" Paige in Yankee Stadium, Jackie Robinson of the
Brooklyn Dodgers, 1948 Harlem Globetrotters pitching staff, and
members of the newly merged Newark Dodgers and Brooklyn Eagles

Printed in the United States of America

*McFarland & Company, Inc., Publishers
Box 611, Jefferson, North Carolina 28640
www.mcfarlandpub.com*

To Dunkin' Daniel Richison,
my basketball court mentor,
and to the memory of Woody Smallwood (1933–1995),
a family friend and a mentor for the ages

Woody Smallwood

New York baseball is really all right,
But you'd be sadly mistaken if you thought it was all white.
There were players of color all around,
The City that gave the fans a thrill,
By playing baseball at a high level,
Like life up on Sugar Hill

—editor Philip Ross, author and historian,
Jamaica, New York

Table of Contents

Acknowledgment

After a week of unseasonably warm and sunny January weather, there was a sudden drop in temperature. That Friday morning, January 26, was cold, foggy, damp and rainy. The sun failed to appear that day and so did a gentleman named Dewitt Mark "Woody" Smallwood.

A native of Newburgh, New York, Smallwood grew up in White Plains, New Rochelle and Buffalo. In high school, he played football and basketball, but baseball was his true love. In 1952, he was signed by Albert "Buster" Haywood to an Indianapolis Clowns contract. Smallwood joined a talented Clowns team that included future home run king Hank Aaron. Woody often recalled how Aaron *"...could make that tin fence in Winston-Salem talk with his line drive hits."* Smallwood also enjoyed playing alongside all stars Jim "Fireball" Cohen and Henry "Speed" Merchant, and Negro League batting champions Len Pigg and Ray Neil.

That season with the Clowns, according to Howe News Bureau, the league's official record-keeper during the 1950s, he hit an even .300. Interviews with teammates often testified that Smallwood had the speed of Rickey Henderson, a gold glove like Ken Griffey, Jr., and Rod Carew's bat control. Many say he was blessed with insane bolting speed, a quick bat and lots of baseball savvy.

The next year, Smallwood joined St. Jean (Quebec), a Pittsburgh Pirates farm team, while Aaron played in Eau Claire (Wisconsin). Mr. Woody returned to the Negro Leagues in 1954 to play with the New York Black Yankees, Birmingham Black Barons and the Philadelphia Stars. When Branch Rickey signed him to a St. Jean contract, Woody humanized the barrier breaking legend by recalling how *"Rickey's suit lapels always had cigar ashes on them."*

Later in the early 1990s, Woody Smallwood became the Negro Leagues Baseball Museum's first president and led a small group of dreamers to a large professional contingent of believers. Under his leadership the Museum reached unprecedented levels of awareness. At many board meetings he would remind us, *"People, we are now in the big leagues."*

As a Special Project Coordinator executive for the High Life Sales Division of the Miller Brewing Company and a former player, Smallwood dedicated his ambitions to building a memorial to the veterans of black baseball. Woody would gladly appear with his gold-headed walking cane and super-shined Stacy Adams footwear, campaigning for corporate funds, speaking at schools, churches, and community organizations on behalf of the NLBM.

A wise man, in dire situations he would often remind us, *"I know what time it is."* In the heat of battle, he encouraged me to reach higher plateaus, saying, *"Larry, you can't fight, unless you are in the ring."* Smallwood always had time to listen to concerns from board members and to make tough decisions in critical situations. He could render presidential decisions from his corporate office, the Museum's office, or from his hang-out, the Madden Shine Parlor, where home-spun wisdom was at a premium.

Woody Smallwood was always a professional, on and off the field. He always started each board meeting on time and with a prayer. Woody ran his meetings with diplomacy and tact. And when appropriate, to emphasize a point, he would drop to a baritone voice like James Earl Jones. Meanwhile, his Billy Dee Williams smile would dilute any anxiety in the room. Even the eloquent John "Buck" O'Neil would look for his marching orders from President Smallwood.

His earthly time has passed, but he is not forgotten. The Museum that he helped birth will be eternally grateful for the time he delightfully shared. For he knew what time it really was!

In Smallwood's home going celebration, his wife Barbara expressed, "I love you, Dewitt, and I'll carry your love in my heart every day, for strength, guidance and courage. It fills me with pride and joy to have had you as my husband."

Preface

New York City, New Jack City and Sugar Hill are names synonymous with life in the city that never sleeps. Sugar Hill was likely named for the sweet life its affluent residents enjoyed during black baseball's heyday during the 1920s, 1930s and 1940s. Roughly bounded by West 155th Street to the north, West 145th Street to the south, Edgecombe Avenue to the east, and Amsterdam Avenue to the west, in Upper Manhattan and known for its distinguished and magnificent row houses and elegant apartments, Sugar Hill is more a state of mind than an actual geographic location.

In the March 27, 1944, edition of *The New Republic*, Langston Hughes wrote about the cultural richness of the neighborhood in his essay "Down Under in Harlem."

> If you are white and are reading this vignette, don't take it for granted that all Harlem is a slum. It isn't. There are big apartment houses up on the hill, Sugar Hill, and up by City College—nice high-rent-houses with elevators and doormen, where [actor] Canada Lee lives, and [Blues musician] W. C. Handy, and the [journalist] George S. Schuylers, and the [civil rights activist] Walter Whites, where colored families send their babies to private kindergartens and their youngsters to [the private] Ethical Culture [Fieldston] School.

Harlem in general, and the Sugar Hill district in particular, was never a slum to renowned painter Aaron Douglas, scholar W. E. B. DuBois, future Supreme Court Justice Thurgood Marshall, politician Adam Clayton Powell, Jr., and singer/actor Paul Robeson, nor to musicians like Count Basie, Cab Calloway, Duke Ellington, and rock n' roll idol Frankie Lymon, along with athletes like pugilist Joe Louis and "Say Hey" Willie Mays.

Sugar Hill was home away from home for visiting Negro League teams, at the Woodside Hotel, at 2424 7th Avenue (near West 141st Street). In the late 1930s, the Count Basie Orchestra, featuring vocalist Billie Holiday, pumped out "Jumpin' at the Woodside" to entertain all fans of the game in the cultural capital of Black America.

Inspired by the 1993 movie *Sugar Hill*, starring Wesley Snipes, Michael Wright, Abe Vigoda, Clarence Williams III, and Theresa Randle, I want to convey the richness and challenges of urban life in New York City with visuals of diamond success. Once home to several professional black baseball teams, today Sugar Hill includes the 12.8-acre Jackie Robinson Park, the Dance Theater of Harlem, the Children's Museum of Art and Storytelling, the Harlem School of Arts, and a state and national landmark, the Hamilton Grange Library.

◆ 1 ◆

Cuban Giants, 1885–1899

The Cuban Giants, who, by the way, are neither giants nor Cubans, but thick-set and brawny colored men, make about as stunning an exhibition as they play great ball, but, outside of that they do more talking, yelling, howling, and bluffing than all the teams in the National League put together. There is a spirit among them which carries the spectators back a good many years in ball-playing. It is one of the best teams in the city to see.—T. Thomas Fortune, *New York Age,* September 5, 1888

In July 1885, the Keystone Athletics, an all-black team organized in Philadelphia by headwaiter Frank P. Thompson, relocated to the Argyle Hotel, in Babylon, New York, to perform before the hotel's guests. That fall, the Athletics merged with the Orions of Philadelphia, and the Manhattans of Washington, D.C., to create New York's Cuban Giants, becoming the country's first African American salaried baseball team. Some sources cite pay of $18 a week for pitchers and catchers, $15 a week for outfielders and $12 a week for infielders.

The following year, 1886, the team was purchased by Walter E. Simpson, who utilized the Chambersburg Grounds in Trenton as their home field. In October of that year, Judge Charles J. Donohue, in New York City, incorporated the team. A few months later, Simpson sold the team to brothers Walter and William Cook. The brothers named S. K. Govern as their manager.

The Cook ownership was brief, as J. M. Bright purchased the club in June of 1887. The 1887 season was pivotal for African American players in organized baseball, and by mid-season, the International League banned teams from signing new contracts with black players. Future Hall of Famer Frank Grant,

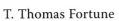

T. Thomas Fortune

like other African American players including George Stovey and brothers Weldy and Fleetwood Walker, faced discrimination on and off the field. Second baseman Grant had worn improvised wooden shin guards at the keystone bag to protect himself from spiking. He was thrown at by pitchers repeatedly, and on several occasions, his own teammates threatened to strike if he continued to play—and sometimes refused to pose for team pictures if he was included.

Despite the social climate of the period, Bright, in 1889, was able to get the Giants into the racially integrated Middle States League of teams from Pennsylvania, Connecticut, New Jersey, Delaware and New York. By mid-season of 1890, the Cubans left Trenton and became the Colored Monarchs of York, Pennsylvania.

The next year, 1891, they joined the Connecticut State League, as the Ansonia (CT) Cuban Giants. This edition of the Cuban Giants displayed the talents of Frank Grant, Sol White and George Stovey. Until the team was sold in 1896, to E. B. Lamar, Jr. of Brooklyn, the stripped-down Giants, under Bright's ownership, was known by a variety of names: Famous Cuban Giants, Genuine Cuban Giants, Original Cuban Giants. Lamar's newer version became the stellar Cuban X-Giants, one of the East Coast's best teams.

In the winter of 1906, the Cuban X-Giants became a charter member of the National Association of Colored Baseball Clubs of the United States and Cuba. The team folded before play started in 1907, never to appear on the diamond again.

Cuban Giants, 1885–1899

UNOFFICIAL COLORED CHAMPIONS—1887, 1888, 1894

League Affiliations

MIDDLE STATES LEAGUE, 1889–1890
CONNECTICUT STATE LEAGUE, 1891

Hall of Famers, Years with Team	Halls of Fame and Induction Years
Frank Grant, 1892–1900	United States 2006
Sol White, 1890–1891, 1893–1894, 1896–1897	United States 2006

Playing Fields

Chambersburg Grounds, Trenton, New Jersey
East State Street Grounds, Trenton, New Jersey
Hertzel's Grove, Trenton, New Jersey
Inlet Park, Atlantic City, New Jersey
Long Island Recreation Grounds, Long Island, NY
Manhattan Field (Polo Grounds), New York, NY

KING SOLOMON "SOL" WHITE—The godfather of early day black baseball was a native of Bellaire, Ohio. This prince of Bellaire played for several New York teams, the Gorhams in 1889, Cuban Giants (1889–1894), Cuban X-Giants (1896–1899, 1901), Columbia Giants (1900), Brooklyn Royal Giants (1910), and Lincoln Giants (1911). Courtesy Jerry Malloy.

THE EDUCATOR—The August 7, 1909, editions of the *Chicago Broad Ax* and the *Indianapolis Freeman* reported, *"Captain White enjoys the reputation of being the only professional Negro player who is a college graduate, having been educated at Wilberforce University, which is the oldest institution in America for the education of Afro-Americans."* Available academic records from Wilberforce for 1895–1896 and 1896–1897 show that the theology major got his sheepskin by taking classes in Reading, Grammar, Geography, Arithmetic, Spelling, U.S. History and Physiology. On a scale of 1 to 10, White earned grades ranging from 8.7 to 9.5. His education paid off. In the late 1920s, the bookish White penned a column for the *New York Amsterdam News*. Courtesy John Thorn.

ARGYLE HOTEL IN BABYLON TOWN & VILLAGE—This 350-room resort hotel was built in 1882, by Long Island Railroad owner Austin Corbin. With a view of the Great South Bay, the site occupied 15 acres, but never exceeded one-third capacity. The hotel closed on October 1, 1897. Seven years later it was dismantled, with the lumber used to build 20 houses on the grounds. Courtesy Babylon Public Library.

Right and below: MARKERS—This marker resides in Argyle Park, which was donated to the Village of Babylon by J. Stanley Foster, Esquire, in 1921. It is still used today for walking and fishing and contains a children's playground. The August 22, 1885, edition of *Babylon's South Side* reported a game between the National Club of Farmingdale and the Athletics of Babylon, won by hotel employees, 29 to one.

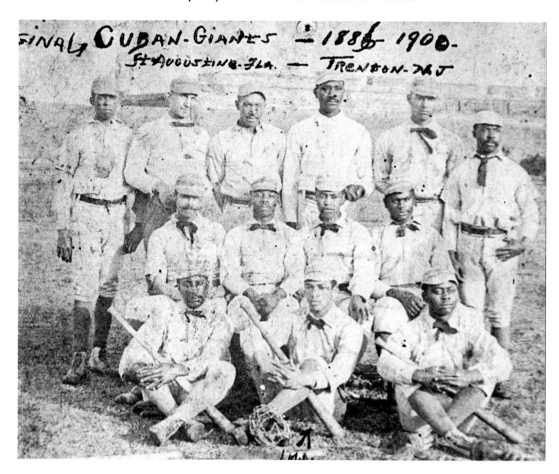

THE ORIGINAL CUBAN GIANTS—In 1885, the Cuban Giants were founded by Frank P. Thompson, a headwaiter at Long Island's Argyle Hotel in Babylon, New York. The African Americans chose the Cuban name to disguise themselves as foreigners as a ruse and to appease their white clientele. This Cuban club eventually moved to Trenton, New Jersey, playing skillful semi-pro and minor league clubs. This photograph was taken in St. Augustine, Florida, the winter home of the Giants before the start of the summer season. Their feature player was lefty George Stovey, top row, second from the right. Stovey later signed with Newark of the International League, in 1887, and won 34 games—a league record that still stands today. This is the only known photograph of Stovey with the club. Courtesy John and Lilian Dabney.

CUBAN GIANTS, 1888—From left to right: (front row) Billy Whyte, George Williams, Abe Harrison, manager S. K. Govern, Ben Boyd, Jack Fry, David Allen; (standing) George Parago, Ben Holmes, Shep Trusty, Arthur Thomas, Clarence Williams, Frank Miller. Sol White, who joined the Giants the following year, wrote, "Their games attracted the attention of baseball writers all over the country, and the Cuban Giants were heralded everywhere as marvels of the baseball world." Courtesy John and Lilian Dabney.

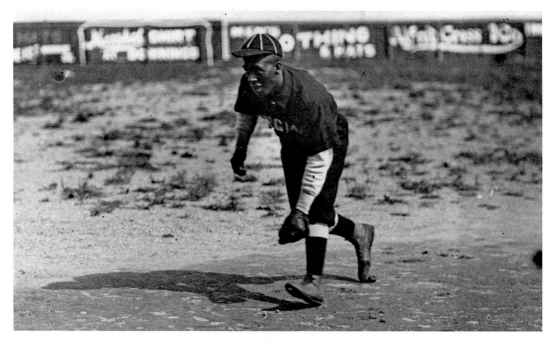

CUBAN X-GIANTS—The golden era of the Cuban Giants came to a close in 1896 when E. B. Lamar signed J. M. Bright's best players and called his team of ex-Cuban Giants, fittingly, the Cuban X-Giants. Thereafter, Bright often called his team the "Original" or "Genuine" Cuban Giants. Danny McClellan sits on the front row, second from the right. In 1903, McClellan pitched the first recorded perfect game by a black pitcher, against the Penn Park Athletic Club of York, Pennsylvania, champions of the Tri-State League.

Opposite, top: HARRY CATO, 1887–1896, SECOND BASEMAN—Cato, a versatile infielder, was a member of the 1887 and 1888 Colored Champion teams. Cato also spent time with the New York Gorhams in 1889 and the Cuban X-Giants in 1893.

Bottom: CLARENCE "CLEM" SAMPSON, 1896–1907, PITCHER—Sampson is remembered for his outstanding games on the mound for a variety of John Bright's teams: the Cuban Giants, the Genuine Cuban Giants, and the Famous Cuban Giants.

JOHN McGRAW—Hall of Fame manager McGraw piloted the New York Giants to ten pennants and three World Series titles from 1902 to 1932. Earlier, in 1901, as manager of the Baltimore Orioles, he attempted to pass a straight-haired, high-cheekboned, café au lait-complexioned player, Charlie Grant (shown at right), as a full-blooded Cherokee. Grant also played for the Cuban X-Giants. Courtesy Dick Clark.

TOKOHOMA—The newly-christened Charlie "Tokohoma" was soon exposed by White Sox president Charles Comiskey. Comiskey had recognized Charles Grant as the former black second baseman of the Columbia Giants. He snitched to league officials, causing Grant to be expelled from the Orioles. Similar attempts by other white managers met with similar fates. Grant also played for the semi-pro New York Black Sox in 1910.

ULYSSES FRANKLIN "FRANK" GRANT, 1889, 1891–1897, 1899, SECOND BASE-
MAN—In 1886, Grant, perhaps the greatest black second baseman of the 19th century,
was described by the *Buffalo Express* as a "Spaniard." That year he hit .325 for Meridien
in the Eastern League. When the Meridien club folded, Grant joined Buffalo of the
higher class International Association and hit even better at .340—third best in the
league. The *Buffalo Courier* summarized Grant's season on January 16, 1887, extolling
"the great Grant, undoubtedly the king of players in that position, as far as the International League is concerned, and the peer of the best of them in the greater organizations. Grant played here last year and is 20 years of age."

The Sunday edition of the *Denver Daily News* reported on April 29, 1888, that
"Grant, the colored second baseman of the Buffalos [*sic*] is the only negro [*sic*] playing
professionally with any club in the different associations. He is a fine tosser, all the
same, and hasn't many superiors among players either white or black. I think he gets
$600 per year for his services, while if he had a white skin, he could easily demand
$2,000."

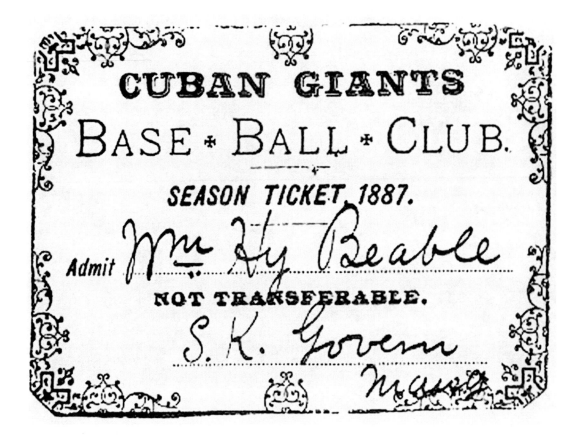

YOUR SEASON TICKET TO GREATNESS!—Cuban Giants manager Stanislaus Kostka "Cos" Govern, whose signature appears on this ticket, was a native of St. Croix in the Virgin Islands. Govern, named after a 16th-century Polish saint, was also a labor organizer, journalist, and Shakespearean actor. The church would remain important throughout Govern's life. According to author and historian Dr. Michael Lomax, Govern was part of the mulatto elite and had an innate ability to conduct business at the most fundamental level—scheduling. He attracted major league clubs with hefty guarantees or percentages, also booking an array of matches with minor league, college, and local club teams.

♦ 2 ♦

Lincoln Stars,
1914–1916

The Stars were a spin-off from the Lincoln Giants founded in 1911 by white boxing promoters Jess and Ed McMahon. Their three-year reign hit its pinnacle in 1915, when the Stars tied the Chicago American Giants, competing for the unofficial Colored World Series title.

The 1915 team was regarded as one of the strongest black teams in the East. The team showcased Cannonball Dick Redding and Howard University grad and dentist Franklin "Doc" Sykes as pitchers, Bill Pierce as catcher, Zack Pettus at first base, Bill Kindle at second base, Sam Mongin at third base, John Henry Lloyd at shortstop, Jude Gans in left field, Spot Poles in center, and Lou Santop in right and as backup catcher. They played a championship series against the Chicago American Giants, but the series ended in controversy. Each team won five games, and after the deciding 11th game was called in the fourth inning with the Stars ahead by a run, it was never completed or replayed. After the series, Lloyd and Gans jumped the Stars to rejoin the American Giants.

Their last season, 1916, was another highlight year as they again faced the Chicago American Giants for the World's Colored Championship. Seven games were played from August 6 through 18. Just before the championship series, Oscar Charleston returned to the Indianapolis ABCs. Despite the absence of Charleston, the Stars took a 3–2 lead in the series, but then lost the final two games.

The Stars failed to field a team in 1917, as players scattered, some forming a semi-pro team called the Pennsylvania Red Caps of New York. The Red Caps competed against professional Negro League teams from 1917 to 1921 and from 1925 through 1935.

The team's Pennsylvania mention was not a state association, but a reference to Penn Station, the extremely busy, main intercity railroad station in New York City, built by the Pennsylvania Railroad from 1901 to 1910. The Red Caps referred to several players who also served as red caps (or porters) at the landmark station.

Hall of Famers, Years with Team	National Halls and Induction Years
Oscar Charleston, 1915–1916	United States 1976
Pop Lloyd, 1915	United States 1977
Louis Santop, 1915–1916	United States 2006

Home Field

Harlem Oval (a.k.a. Lenox Oval or the Bronx Oval) at 142nd Street & Lenox Avenue, New York, NY. Seating capacity: 2,600.

JOHN HENRY "POP" LLOYD, 1915, SHORTSTOP—The *Indianapolis Freeman* of 1910 reported, *"Lloyd, former second baseman of the Philadelphia Giants, is considered by every manager in the country to be a wonder of the 20th century. He contains a ball team within himself."* Nineteen fifteen was Lloyd's only season with the Stars. A retired Lloyd (left) is shown with former MVP winner and popular Hall of Fame first baseman Jimmie Foxx.

WALTER "BIG TRAIN" JOHNSON—On October 11, 1914, the Stars faced Washington Senators ace Walter "Big Train" Johnson at Lenox Oval. Johnson was pitching for the New York Fire Department. Johnson give up five hits and struck out six Stars, as rookie "Gunboat" Thompson struck out 13 smoke eaters. The Stars won, 2–0. Johnson traditionally left opposing batters standing in their tracks. With 416 major league victories, he ranks second on the all-time win list behind Cy Young. He compiled an unbelievable 2.17 career ERA, tossed a record 110 shutouts, and pitched 56 consecutive scoreless innings in 1913. In 1936, the Big Train was among Cooperstown's first class of Hall of Fame electees. Despite his accolades, the Big Train seldom achieved a choo-choo against black teams. Courtesy Dick Clark.

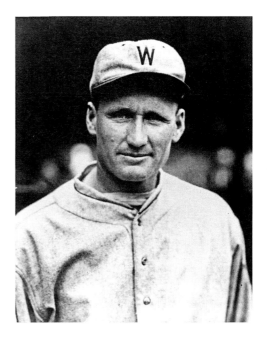

FRANK "RED ANT" WICKWARE, 1916, PITCHER— Back on October 5, 1913, before 6,000 fans, Wickware defeated future Hall of Fame pitcher Walter "Big Train" Johnson, 1–0. The game was halted after five innings because of darkness. The game had been delayed because Wickware and the Mohawk Colored Giants of Schenectady refused to take the field until their back salaries from owner Bill Wernecke were paid. Courtesy Frank Keetz.

CLAUDE CECIL "HOOKS" JOHNSON, 1916, THIRD & SECOND BASEMAN—Johnson started his pro career in 1916 with the Lincoln Stars. For the next 12 years, he commanded play around second base and third base for the Cleveland Tate Stars, Harrisburg Giants, Birmingham Black Barons, Memphis Red Sox, Nashville Elite Giants and Pittsburgh Crawfords.

SPOTTSWOOD "SPOT" POLES, 1923, CENTER FIELDER—Legend has it, Poles could go from home to first faster than three Mississippis. The bowlegged Poles often hit for a high average. In 1918, he joined the military and served in France with the 369th Infantry Regiment, also known as the Harlem Hellfighters. As a sergeant he earned five battle stars and a Purple Heart. SDN-058616, Chicago Daily News Collection, Chicago History Museum.

LOUIS SANTOP, 1915–1916, CATCHER, RIGHT FIELDER—Santop also played for the Lincoln Giants (1911–1914) and the Brooklyn Royal Giants (1914–1919). When Santop passed away in 1942 Buster Miller wrote in the *New York Age* that *"Acknowledged as the greatest catcher of his time, Santop was probably a better batter than receiver. There are several catchers today, notably Josh Gibson, Larry Brown, Frank Duncan and Biz Mackey, who are better behind the plate than Santop ever was, but few can equal his prowess with the willow."*

OSCAR McKINLEY CHARLES-
TON, 1915–1916, OUTFIELDER—
Charleston, the most prolific hitter of his era, was the mainstay
of the Indianapolis ABC's. Often
contracted to play with other
clubs to beef up their offensive
attack, the great Oscar seldom
failed. Some historians consider
him the greatest player in black
baseball history. Charleston,
here in his Almendares gear (of
the Cuban League), was elected
to the National Baseball Hall of
Fame in 1976.

♦ 3 ♦

Brooklyn Royal Giants, 1905–1927

The Brooklyn Royal Giants were founded in 1905 by cafe owner J. W. Connor. Connor owned the Royal Café, on 176 Myrtle Avenue, a night club called the Brooklyn Royal Garden, and the Porter's Club. With less than mass appeal, Connor used the Royal Giants to advertise his eatery and dance hall.

In 1907, the Royal Giants joined the National Association of Colored Base Ball Clubs of the United States and Cuba. The league included the Philadelphia Giants, Cuban X-Giants, Cuban Stars of Havana and Cuban Giants. Walter Schlichter of the Philadelphia Giants was elected president, with J. M. Bright of the Cuban Giants as treasurer, organizer Nat Strong as secretary, and Connor as vice-president.

During the league's three years of operation, the Royal Giants were declared colored champions by *Sporting Life* magazine and the *Indianapolis Freeman* in its second and third seasons. Connor eventually sold the club to Nat Strong, the league's booking agent, in July of 1913.

Hall of Famers, Years with Team	*National Halls and Induction Years*
Jose Mendez, 1908	Cuba 1939, United States 2006
Smokey Joe Williams, 1924	United States 1999
John Henry "Pop" Lloyd, 1918–1920	United States 1977
Louis Santop, 1915–1919	United States 2006
King Solomon "Sol" White, 1910	United States 2006
Oliver Marcell, 1918–1919, 1930	Cuba 2007

Eastern Colored League Standings

Year	*W/L*	*Place, Games Behind First Place*
1923	18–18	3rd place, 7½ games
1924	16–26	6th place, 17½ games
1925	13–20	5th place, 19½ games
1926	7–20	team folded in mid-season
1927	15–31	last place, 17½ games

Home Fields

Harlem Oval (a.k.a. Lenox Oval or the Bronx Oval) at 142nd Street & Lenox Avenue, New York, NY. Seating capacity: 2,600.

Dexter Park (a.k.a. Bushwick Park, or Sterling Oval), on the north side of Jamaica Avenue between Elderts Lane (now Dexter Court) and 76th Street in Woodhaven Section, near the border of Brooklyn & Queens. Seating capacity: 15,400.

WALTER THOMAS BALL, 1905, 1913, CENTERFIELDER AND PITCHER—At the turn of the century, he was ranked with Rube Foster and Danny McClellan as the top aces of early day baseball. Perhaps his greatest season was 1909 while with the Leland Giants, when he lost only one of 25 league games. In 1905, Ball played the first half of the season for the Brooklyn Royal Giants. During the last half of the season, he was back playing for the Chicago Union Giants, reportedly winning 48 straight games. SDN-055357, Chicago Daily News Collection, Chicago History Museum.

WAYNE CARR, 1921, 1927, PITCHER—A solid performer on any pitching staff, Carr started his career in the Negro Leagues with the St. Louis Giants in 1920. He is shown here in 1922 with the Indianapolis ABCs. He played for the Brooklyn Royal Giants in 1921 and 1927. Other teams to enjoy his talents were Atlantic City Bacharach Giants, Wilmington Potomacs, Newark Stars and Baltimore Black Sox. Carr closed out his career with New York's Lincoln Giants in 1928, before going on to manage the Miami Giants in 1934.

Jose Mendez
the Black Mathewson.

JOSE "THE BLACK DIAMOND" DE LA MENDEZ, 1908, PITCHER—Known in Cuba as "El Diamante Negro" or The Black Diamond, Mendez was in the inaugural induction class of the Cuban Baseball Hall of Fame in 1939. After his only season with the Royal Giants, the small dude with a big-time fastball, thrown from a rocking chair motion, cemented his legendary spot in history against the Cincinnati Reds in the Cuban Winter League. After seeing Mendez beat his aces, Christy Mathewson and Nap Rucker, New York Giants manager John McGraw boasted, "I have just seen the greatest pitcher of all time." As a member of the Almendares Blues, Mendez pitched 25 consecutive scoreless innings in three appearances, capturing three wins over the major leaguers. He struck out 24, giving up eight hits and three walks.

GEORGE "DIBO" JOHNSON, 1918, CENTER FIELDER—Johnson was an outstanding player with power, speed, and a strong throwing arm, and was an excellent outfielder. You would normally find him in the cleanup spot of any batting order. Johnson, from San Marcos, Texas, also played for the New York Lincoln Giants in 1926 and 1927.

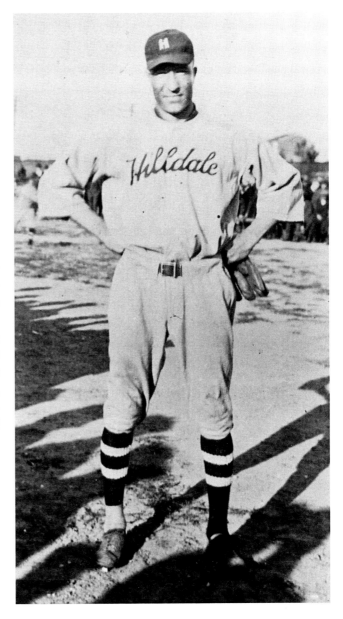

LOUIS "TOP" SANTOP, 1915–1919, CATCHER—The Tyler, Texas, native's full name was Louis Santop Loftin. William E. Clark of the *New York Age* wrote, *"Santop, the 'Big Bertha' of baseball wasn't the greatest receiver in the world, but he was a wonderful drawing card and the hardest hitting catcher I ever saw. He was a forerunner of Babe Ruth and was feared by all pitchers especially when men were on base."* With a body that would shame Samson, his physical presence scared the daylights out of pitchers.

Opposite, top: 1914 SQUAD—This picture was taken at Wallace's Ridgewood Grounds in Long Island. The Royal Giants laid claim to the unofficial Colored Championship back in 1909, by defeating the Cuban Stars in the best of five, winning three games against one loss, at the Bronx Oval. Courtesy Dr. Bennett Rosner.

Bottom: 1917 TEAM—This picture was taken at Washington Park in Brooklyn. From left to right (bottom row): Louis Santop (sporting a World Colored Champion jersey), William "Duckbreast" Handy, Ernest Gatewood, Joe Hewitt, John Henry "Little Pitch" Harvey; (middle row) Andrew "Stringbean" Williams, Charles Earle, William Kindle, Pearl Webster, Johnny Pugh; (top row) owner Nat Strong, Frank "Doc" Sykes, business manager Max Rosner. Courtesy Dr. Bennett Rosner.

RAMIRO "ROME" RAMIREZ, 1920, OUTFIELDER—The Cuban center fielder was a natural leadoff hitter. A student of the game, Ramirez later managed the New York Black Yankees in 1936. He played roughly 20 years in the black leagues for the New York Cuban Stars, All Cubans, New York Bacharach Giants, Baltimore Black Sox and Havana Red Sox. Courtesy Luis Alvelo.

Left: "SMOKEY" JOE WILLIAMS, 1924, PITCHER—Everybody called him Smokey, for his fastball filled nostrils with the sizzling aroma of burnt horsehide. At six feet, five inches tall, he was a towering inferno of a pitcher. *"Joe didn't wind up. He pitched just like Don Larsen, right from the shoulder,"* claimed pitcher Sam Streeter. This was Williams' only season with the Royal Giants. Courtesy Jeff Eastland.

Right: JOHN HENRY "POP" LLOYD, 1918–1920, SHORTSTOP—Approaching the age of 35, Lloyd signed with the Brooklyn Royal Giants as player-manager in 1918. After three seasons with the Royal Giants, en route to Cooperstown, Lloyd made a pit stop with the Columbus (Ohio) Buckeyes in 1921. Lloyd, now 37, led the new Columbus franchise in games played, hits, doubles and stolen bases, meanwhile hitting a solid .336.

OLIVER HAZZARD "GHOST" MAR-CELL, 1918–1919, 1930, THIRD BASE-MAN—The New Orleans ghost was a fielding gem who could go to his right or left with equal facility, coming up with breathtaking plays on bunts. The fearless fielder became known for charging in on batters when the ball was pitched. With his rapid reflexes, he could snag line drives before they hit the unmanicured infield turf. Fans called him the ghost because his frightening speed, as the French would say, je ne sais quoi. Now he's here, now he's gone. However, his talent was no mystery, for his play was spooktacular. For more than a decade, Marcell haunted the opposition. Marcell also played for the New York Lincoln Giants from 1923 to 1925. Courtesy The Rucker Archive.

MERVEN JOHN "RED" RYAN, 1919, PITCHER—The diminutive Brooklyn native was in great demand because of his wide assortment of pitches: fastball, knuckler, forkball and curve. Ryan also pitched for the Lincoln Stars in 1916 and later for the Lincoln Giants in 1928 and 1930. Courtesy The Rucker Archive.

RICHARD "CANNONBALL" DICK REDDING, 1916, 1918, 1923–1932, PITCHER— Redding, pictured with Smokey Joe Williams on the left, was the ace of the Royal Giants' pitching staff for several years. Hall of Famer Buck Leonard recalled Redding as a "nice fellow, easy going. He never argued, never cursed, never smoked as I recall; I never saw him take a drink." "He was also temperamental," claimed Judy Johnson, another Hall of Famer. "If he lost a game, he'd buy a new glove. As if the glove had anything to do with it." Redding and Williams were considered the country's top black pitchers during the deadball era.

JESSE JAMES "MOUNTAIN MAN" HUBBARD, 1917, 1919–1926, PITCHER, RIGHT FIELDER—Hubbard signed his first pro contract with the Royal Giants in 1917. The rookie was drafted into the U.S. Army the following year and pitched for Fort Dix in New Jersey. Returning in 1919, he joined the toughest pitching staff in the East with Smokey Joe Williams and Cannonball Dick Redding. The light-skinned fellow once pitched two shutouts against the New York Giants, providing some temptation for owners to break the color barrier. Hubbard was from Bering, Texas. Courtesy Kimshi Productions.

BABE RUTH WHIFFS—The Great Bambino hit 54 home runs in 1920, but failed to connect against Pud Flournoy in a post-season contest. To pick up a little extra cash, white teams often played black teams after the season. Flournoy struck out Babe Ruth twice in a game played on October 7, 1920. It has been reported that, for a brief period, Ruth as a child lived at 409 Edgecombe Avenue (originally the Colonial Parkway Apartments) in the Sugar Hill district.

WILLIS JEFFERSON "PUD," "JESSE" FLOURNOY, 1923–1928, PITCHER—Pud was no puddin' head. The big left-hander from Monticello, Georgia, had all the tools, a great fastball, excellent curve and superb control. On August 14, 1932, in Fairview, New Jersey, while pitching for the Baltimore Black Sox, Flourney attempted an iron man stunt. He pitched the first game of a doubleheader against the semi-pro Camden team, losing 2–1, and pitched the first four innings of the second game, which ended in a 1–1 tie.

ZACHARY M. "SMILEY" CLAYTON, 1938, FIRST BASEMAN—This was Clayton's only season with the Royal Giants. He later played for the New York Black Yankees in 1943 and 1944. He also helped lead the 1939 New York Rens to a World Basketball Championship and the 1943 Washington Bears to the same title. In 1949, Clayton, seen at right with unidentified teammates, became the first black man to receive a referee's boxing license from the state of Pennsylvania. In 1952, he became the first African American to referee a heavyweight title fight—Ezzard Charles vs. Jersey Joe Walcott in their fourth meeting. However, he is best remembered for officiating the "Rumble in the Jungle" bout in Zaire, between George Foreman and Muhammad Ali. The multitalented man began his humble career in 1931 with the semi-pro [Louis] Santop's Broncos at the age of 14.

Above: 1943 WASHINGTON BEARS—In 1943, Charles "Tarzan" Cooper (far left), John Isaacs (fourth from left), William "Pop" Gates (fifth from left), and Zach Clayton (third from right) led the Washington Bears to a 41–0 record. In the championship game of the World Professional Basketball Championship tournament, they defeated the Oshkosh All-Stars, 43–31.

Left: CLINTON CYRUS "HAWK" THOMAS, 1920, SECOND BASEMAN—He was discovered by the stellar John Henry "Pop" Lloyd while playing in Columbus, Ohio. Lloyd signed him to play in 1920 with his Royal Giants. When Lloyd became manager of the Columbus Buckeyes the next season, he took Thomas with him. He eventually moved to the outfield and became one of the league's best fly hawks, thus his nickname. He was a key member of the 1924 and 1925 Hilldale championship teams. Some of his final seasons were spent with the New York Black Yankees, earning him the tag "The Black Joe DiMaggio," because of his all-around play.

Cuban Stars (East),
1917–1932

Also known as the New York Cuban Stars, this team was founded by Alex Pompez.

Hall of Famers, Years with Team	National Halls and Induction Years
Luis Arango, 1931–1932	Cuba 1986
Bernardo Baro, 1923–1930	Cuba 1945
Pelayo Chacon, 1923–1927, 1930–1931	Cuba 1949
Alejandro "Filete" Crespo, 1926–1927, 1933	Cuba 1962
Martin Dihigo, 1923–1927, 1930	Cuba 1951, Mexico 1964, United States 1977
Isidro Fabre, 1923–1934	Cuba 1957
Jose Fernandez, 1923–1934	Cuba 1965
Cando Lopez, 1931–1932, 1934	Cuba 1984
Armando Marsans, 1923	Cuba 1939
Pablo "Champion" Mesa, 1923–1927	Cuba 1964
Emilio Navarro, 1928–1929	Puerto Rico 1992
Alejandro Oms, 1923–1932	Cuba 1944
Luis Mulo Padron, 1923	Cuba 1943
Eustaquio Pedroso, 1926, 1930	Cuba 1962
Alex Pompez, owner	Cuba 1997, United States 2006
Bartolo Portuando, 1923–1927	Cuba 1985
Julio Rojo, 1917–1919	Cuba 1984
Tetelo Vargas, 1927–1929	Puerto Rico 1992

Standings

Eastern Colored League

Year	W/L	Place, Games Behind First Place
1923	23–17	2nd place, 4½
1924	17–31	7th place, 20
1925	15–26	6th place, 21½
1926	28–21	4th place, 3½
1927	33–32	3rd place, 8
1928	4–3	league folded in mid-season

American Negro League

Year	W/L	Place, Games Behind First Place
1929	15–39	last place, 26 games behind

East-West League (abbreviated season)
1932   12–15   no final printed standings

Home Field, 1923–1929

Dyckman Oval, bounded by Nagel Avenue (NW), Academy Street (SW), Tenth Street (SE), and West 204th Street (NE), Henry Hudson Parkway and Dyckman Street. Located near Harlem Ship Canal in the Inwood section of Manhattan, near the northern tip of the island. Seating capacity: 10,000.

Above: DYCKMAN OVAL—In 1930, Alex Pompez installed lights at Dyckman Oval, making it the first ballpark in New York equipped for night time enjoyment. Author Michael Benson wrote, "One of the most beautiful locations in Manhattan, the Oval is on a low plain, the only flat land for miles, surrounded by rocky and woody hills, with the blue span of the Henry Hudson Bridge crossing the gorge of the Spuyten David Creek to the Bronx, beyond left field."

Left: GONZALO ALEJANDRO "ALEX" POMPEZ, OWNER, VICE-PRESIDENT OF THE NEGRO NATIONAL LEAGUE—The native of Key West, Florida, was a powerful negotiator and key figure, along with Rube Foster, in the making of the first Colored World Series in 1924. Instrumental in creating the Latino pipeline of talent into the United States, Pompez was named to the 1971 Blue Ribbon Committee by Commissioner Bowie Kuhn to consider Negro Leagues veterans for Cooperstown immortality. The one-time Harlem numbers king, he served on the committee until his death in March 1974, helping to elect Satchel Paige (1971), Josh Gibson and Buck Leonard (1972), Monte Irvin (1973) and James "Cool Papa" Bell (1974).

MARTIN MAGDALENO DIHIGO, 1923–1927, 1930, PITCHER & OUTFIELDER—
Dihigo started his career with the barnstorming Cuban Stars of the newly organized
Eastern Colored League (ECL). He started out as a first baseman under owner Alex
Pompez. Another first baseman, Hall of Famer Buck Leonard, claimed: *"Dihigo was the
best all-around baseball player I have ever seen. He could run, hit, throw, think, pitch
and manage. He both knew the game and could play it. I was in the game for 23 years
and I never saw anyone better than he was."*

ALEJANDRO "EL CABALLERO" OMS (1917, 1922–1932) AND PABLO "CHAMPION" MESA (1921–1927), OUTFIELDERS—Here are two-thirds of the great Cuban Stars outfield, minus Hall of Famer Oscar Charleston. Noted as a great outfielder with power to all fields, Oms had a reputation as a gentleman (caballero) on and off the field. Mesa was known as an excellent bunter, fast on the bases and an excellent hitter with gap power.

PABLO MESA, OSCAR CHARLESTON AND ALEJANDRO OMS, OUTFIELDERS FOR SANTA CLARA 1923/1924—Pablo "Champion" Mesa and Alejandro Oms also teamed with another Hall of Famer, Oscar Charleston. This Santa Clara trio from the 1923–1924 Leopardos is considered the greatest Cuban team of all time. Their 11½-game margin of victory is the largest in Cuban League play. Oms was selected to the Cuban Hall of Fame in 1944, with Mesa joining him 20 years later in 1964.

Right: ALEJANDRO "WALLA WALLA" OMS, 1917, 1922–32, OUTFIELDER—Oms represented the N.Y. Cubans in the third (1935) East-West All-Star Game. The flashy center fielder would give the fans a buzz by catching fly balls behind this back. An outstanding hitter, the Santa Clara native hit over .300 a dozen times, eight times consecutively. Oms ranks second all-time, with a career batting average of .345, to Cristobal Torriente. Courtesy Kimshi Productions.

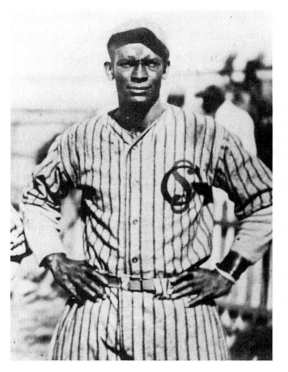

DOMINGO JULIO "CLOWN" ROJO, 1917–1919, CATCHER—Displaying the Santa Clara colors, Rojo was one of the best Cuban catchers in the early days of the Negro Leagues. Rojo played most of his 15-year career around New York, with the Lincoln Giants and the Havana Stars. He also played for the Baltimore Black Sox, where Dick Powell, former business manager of the Baltimore Elite Giants, saw him play. Powell thought the underrated Rojo was a superior receiver to his own backstops, Biz Mackey and Roy Campanella. Courtesy Kimshi Productions.

BARTOLOME PORTUONDO, 1916, 1923–1927, THIRD BASEMAN—Portuondo was selected to the Cuban Professional Baseball Hall of Fame in 1985. Portuondo also played for the western Cuban Stars, based out of Cincinnati from 1917 to 1918. An above average hitter, he was best known for his speed on the base paths and as an excellent infielder. Portuondo is shown here in his Habana Reds uniform. Courtesy The Rucker Archive.

ISIDRO "PAPI" FABRE, 1918–1929, PITCHER—Fabre pitched more than 20 years in the Negro Leagues, closing out his career with the N.Y. Cubans in 1939. The five-foot-six hurler was known for his superb control and finesse on the mound. Teammate Alejandro "Felite" Crespo once revealed, "He'd always pretend to spit [on the baseball]. Sometimes he would, sometimes he didn't."

JOSE MARIA "CUSO" FERNANDEZ, SR., 1916–1934, CATCHER—An outstanding catcher for the Stars and later the New York Cubans. An excellent receiver with a strong arm, he was only an average hitter at the plate. Fernandez later managed the Cubans to their only Negro Leagues world championship in 1947, over the Cleveland Buckeyes. He also managed the All Cubans in the Cuban Winter Leagues during the 1945–1946 season. His son Pepe was also a catcher with the New York Cubans, 1948–1950.

JUAN ESTEBAN "TETELO" VARGAS, 1927–1931, OUTFIELDER—In 1923, Tetelo played with his two brothers on the Escogido club in Santo Domingo. Considered one of the top players to come out of the Dominican Republic, Vargas played in three East-West All-Star Games. Vargas also played for the New York Cubans (1941–1944). Courtesy Luis Alvelo.

ARMANDO MARSANS, 1923, OUTFIELDER—Sporting his Almendares Blues uniform, Marsans also starred in the major leagues for the Cincinnati Reds, the St. Louis Browns and the New York Yankees from 1911 to 1918. He also appeared with the St. Louis Terriers of the Federal League, 1914–1915. In 1911, the Reds had raised the hopes of black athletes by signing Marsans and Rafael Almeida. The *New York Age* said, "Now that the first shock is over it would not be surprising to see a Cuban a few shades darker … breaking the professional ranks … it would then be easier for colored players who are citizens of this country to get into fast company." The Reds quickly countered that Marsans and Almeida were "genuine Caucasians," and the artificial, but very authentic, color barrier was firmly entrenched. After compiling a .269 batting average in eight major league seasons, the man from Matanzas, Cuba, joined the Stars, at age 35, for one final season. Courtesy Kimshi Productions.

OSCAR J. LEVIS, 1921– 1929, 1931–1934, PITCHER— Originally thought to be from Cuba, the Panamanian is thought to be the first player from that country to play in the Negro Leagues. It has been reported that his best pitch was the wet one. The lefty Levis compiled a 48–38 won-lost record in the Cuban Winter Leagues, from 1922 to 1932. Courtesy Kimshi Productions.

MARTIN DIHIGO, 1923–1927, 1930, UTILITY— The Cuban Stars called several ballparks home field. On May 9, 1927, they played as the home team in Richmond, Virginia, against the Hilldale Club from Philadelphia. On this day, Dihigo homered three times and singled in four at-bats. Two of his home runs were grand slams, as he drove in nine runs. The Stars defeated the Hilldales, 12–7.

EMILIO "MILLITO" NAVARRO, 1928–1929, INFIELDER—In 1928, Navarro was the first Puerto Rican to play in the Negro Leagues. The diminutive infielder had great hands and was an excellent leadoff hitter. Born in Patillas in 1905, the always youthful "Millito" could still touch his toes and dance a jig on request, after reaching the century mark. Navarro died in 2011 at the age of 105. He was named to the Puerto Rican Hall of Fame in 1992. Courtesy Wayne Stivers.

♦ 5 ♦

Lincoln Giants,
1911–1930

The team was founded by brothers Jess (father of Vincent, founder of the World Wide Wrestling Federation) and Ed McMahon in 1911. The McMahon brothers originally hired manager Sol White to kick-start the team, because of White's previous success with the champion Philadelphia Giants. White signed superstars Pop Lloyd, Spot Poles, and backstop Lou Santop to catch Smokey Joe Williams and Cannonball Dick Redding. Midway through the first year, White was replaced by Pop Lloyd. The new, high-octane line-up produced unofficial Eastern championships for the next three years, 1911, 1912 and 1913.

The brothers sold their interests to James (Jim) J. Keenan in 1914. When the Eastern Colored League (ECL) was formed in 1923, the Giants became charter members. Despite having some talented players, they only had one winning season during the ECL's duration (1923–1928). After independent play in 1930, they folded, resurfacing two years later as the New York Black Yankees.

James Keenan's office was at 505 W. 137th St., New York, New York.

No future major league players.

Hall of Famers, Years with Team	Halls of Fame and Induction Years
Pop Lloyd, 1911–1915, 1926–1930	United States 1977
Esteban Montalvo, 1927	Cuba 1964
Luis "El Mulo" Padrone, 1915	Cuba 1943
Louis Santop, 1911–1914, 1917	United States 2006
Turkey Stearnes, 1930	United States 2000
Ben Taylor, 1912	United States 2006
Sol White, manager, 1911	United States 2006
Smokey Joe Williams, 1912–1923, 1925	United States 1999

Standings

Eastern Colored League

Year	W/L	Place, Games Behind First
1923	16–22	5th place, 10½
1924	32–25	3rd place, 9
1925	7–39	7th place, 32

Year	W/L	Place, Games Behind First
1926	19–22	5th place, 8½
1927	12–18	did not finish the season
1928	5–5	league folded

American Negro League

1929	40–26	2nd place, 7 games behind

Home Fields

Catholic Protectory Oval in the Bronx at East Tremont Avenue & Unionport Road, in the Parkchester section of the East Bronx. Seating capacity: 12,000.

Harlem Oval (a.k.a. Lenox Oval or Bronx Oval), at 142nd Street & Lenox Avenue. Seating capacity: 2,600.

Olympic Field at East 138th (North) & East 135th (South) Streets, Madison (East) & Fifth (West) Avenues. Centrally located near the Hotel Theresa and the Woodside Hotel, plus the Lafayette and Apollo Theatres. Seating capacity: 5,000. Currently the site of the Riverton Apartments.

1911 GIANTS—From left to right: (front row) Phil Bradley, Harry Buckner, Bill Francis and George Wright; (top row) Dan McClellan, Pop Lloyd, Spot Poles, Tom Johnson, Sol White (in suit), Dick Redding, Louis Santop, Jude Gans and Pete Booker. On October 8, McClellan faced "Big Train" Johnson, who was pitching for the All-Leaguers. Johnson held the Giants to six hits and three runs, as McClellan's team lost, 5–3. Johnson fanned 14, while McClellan whiffed nine men.

Right: The *New York Age* advertised this matchup between the Giants and the Washington Potomacs in 1924. The Lincoln club won the first game, 7–3, and lost the second to the Potomacs, 9–4.

BASEBALL
DOUBLE HEADER

Sunday, June 22, at 2 P. M.

Eastern Colored League
LINCOLN GIANTS

vs.

Washington Potomacs

at

The Catholic Protectory Oval

Take Bronx Subway to 177th Street and Tremont Avenue Car to gate.

Below: 1912 TEAM at Olympic Field at 136th Street and Fifth Avenue—From left to right: (front row, seated) Louis Santop, Smokey Joe Williams, mascot Hutchinson, Cannonball Dick Redding, Zack Pettus, and Charlie Bradford; (middle row, #6) Ashby Dunbar (kneeling); (top row) Bill Francis, Pete Booker, Pop Lloyd, George Wright, and Spot Poles. This team won a reported 108 games against 12 losses. On June 16, Redding struck out 24 batters to break the professional record of 19 held by Charlie Sweeney of Providence, set back in the 1880s.

"SMOKEY" JOE WILLIAMS, 1911–1923, PITCHER—On October 28, 1912, Williams shut out the New York Giants, 6–0, at Olympic Field. He held the National League champs to just four hits, striking out nine men. Two years later, on October 18, he faced off against Rube Marquard, the Giants' number three ace. Williams struck out 12, scattering five hits, while Marquard struck out 14 Lincolnites, surrendering three stingy hits. The game ended in a 1–1 tie, called on account of darkness.

RICHARD "CANNONBALL DICK" REDDING, 1911–1916, PITCHER—Aside from hurler John Donaldson, Cannonball Dick Redding may be the best pitcher from black baseball not in the National Baseball Hall of Fame. Redding is credited with two no-hitters, in 1912 and 1920. Redding also pitched two games on the same day on four occasions, winning seven of eight contests.

POP LLOYD, 1911–1915, 1926–1930, SECOND BASE, MANAGER—Manager Lloyd wrote the *New York Age* in 1913 that his Giants were in Havana, playing for the Fe club, with Cannonball Dick Redding, Smokey Joe Williams, Spot Poles, Jude Gans and Bill Francis in tow. Known as a man of his word, "Pop" guaranteed payment to his players on the 1st and the 15th of every month for the remainder of the season.

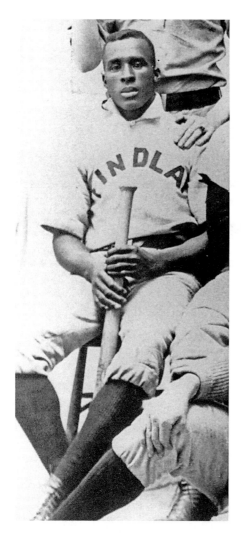 

Left: GRANT "HOME RUN" JOHNSON, 1912–1914, SECOND BASEMAN, SHORT-STOP—Johnson and Bud Fowler were co-founders of the powerhouse Page Fence Giants, out of Adrian, Michigan. He was christened "Home Run" for his outstanding hitting during the deadball era. According to historian and author Ray Nemec, Grant Johnson got his nickname in 1894, when he blasted 60 home runs for the Findlay (Ohio) Sluggers. One of the highlights of Johnson's career was averaging .319 in five seasons in the Cuban Winter League. Courtesy Dick Clark.

Right: DAVE "LEFTY" BROWN, 1923–1925, PITCHER—Formerly of the Chicago American Giants, Brown jumped to the Giants when the Eastern Colored League was formed in 1923. Brown's pitching repertoire included an excellent curve and sinker, along with some top-end speed. After the 1924 season, manager and future Hall of Famer Ben Taylor named Brown and Nip Winters as being "without doubt ... our greatest left-handers." Brown stayed with the club until 1925, when the FBI sought him as a suspect in a murder investigation. Brown disappeared, occasionally resurfacing under an alias for a few upper Midwest teams.

DETECTIVE DIVISION
CIRCULAR No. 5
JULY 23, 1925

POLICE DEPARTMENT
CITY OF NEW YORK

PLEASE POST IN A
CONSPICUOUS PLACE

Police Authorities are Requested to Post this Circular for the Information of Police Officers and File a Copy of it for Future Reference

WANTED FOR MURDER

DAVE BROWN (Negro)

DESCRIPTION—Age, 28 years; height, 5 feet, 11 inches; weight, 165 pounds; seal-brown colored skin; kinky hair; very erect. He is a professional ball player and pitched for the Lincoln Giants up to the time of the crime. He may be found playing with some other colored baseball club.

Shot and killed Benjamin Adair in front of 69 West 135th Street, this City, April 28, 1925. He has been indicted for this crime and a bench warrant issued for his arrest.

If located, arrest and hold as a fugitive from justice and advise the Detective Division.

Kindly search your prison records as this man may be serving a sentence for some minor offense.

Telephone 3100 Spring

RICHARD E. ENRIGHT,
Police Commissioner.

Dave Brown wanted poster.

1915/1916 SQUAD IN PALM BEACH, FLORIDA—To pick up some extra currency during the winter, some teams re-organized for play in warmer climates. From left to right: (front row) Pete Hill, Knux James, Dick Wallace, Spot Poles; (middle row) Jesse Barber, Dicta Johnson, manager Joe Williams (with cigar), Zach Pettus, Bill Francis; (top row) Jesse Barber, Dick Redding, Pop Lloyd, Jud Gans, Louis Santop and Leroy Grant. The *Palm Beach Weekly Review* (2-19-1916) reported that wealthy families, "Astors, Vanderbilts, Morgans and hundreds of others, who never see a ball game outside of Palm Beach are rooting hard for their favorite team, the Breakers [in the Florida State League]." Courtesy Reid Poles.

PETER WASHINGTON, 1925, OUT-FIELDER—In his only year with the Lincolnites, he batted .300. Washington was considered one of the top fly chasers in the league. He also played for the Baltimore Black Sox and the Wilmington (DE) and Washington (DC) Potomacs, during his 14-year career.

GEORGE "TUBBY" SCALES, 1923–1929, SECOND, THIRD BASEMAN, SHORTSTOP—Tubby was a rare power-hitting second baseman who loved hanging curve balls. With the creation of the Eastern Colored League in 1923, he joined the Lincoln club. In seven seasons with the Giants, he always hit over .300. In 1932, Scales became manager of the newly organized New York Black Yankees. Scales is shown here in a Homestead (PA) Grays uniform.

ESTABAN MONTALVO, 1927, OUT-FIELDER, FIRST BASEMAN—During the early 1920s, Montalvo was known for his home run power and high batting averages with Tinti Molina's Cuban Stars of the Negro National League (NNL). In a raid between the NNL and the Eastern Colored League teams, the Lincoln Giants enticed Montalvo to come east. His only year there, 1927, was not up to his standards, and Montalvo returned to the Cuban Stars. Two years later, he succumbed to tuberculosis. Courtesy Kimshi Productions.

JESSE "NIP" WINTERS, 1928, PITCHER—Baseball experts agree that he was one of the finest southpaws in black baseball history. During the 1920s, he was rated as one of the most consistent pitchers in the league. *"Smokey* [Joe Williams] *and Nip Winters both had long arms. It looked like they were handing the ball to the catcher. When they delivered the ball, it was on you before you knew it,"* remembered sportswriter Sam Lacy. Courtesy Kimshi Productions.

JOHN CHRISTOPHER BECKWITH, 1929–1930, SHORTSTOP—One of blackball's greatest home run hitters, *"Beckwith could hit as hard as Gibson but he wouldn't hit as regular [with regularity],"* praised pitcher Sam Streeter. The average fielding shortstop was always atop the leader board each season in home runs, RBIs, batting average and slugging percentage. Big Beck later played for the 1933 and 1934 N.Y. Black Yankees.

Left: JACOB RUPPERT JR.—He built Yankee Stadium in 1923 and eventually turned the Yankees into perennial winners. During his 24 years of ownership, Ruppert acquired more than a dozen future Hall of Famers, including Frank "Home Run" Baker, Earle Combs, Bill Dickey, Joe DiMaggio, Lou Gehrig, Lefty Gomez, Joe Gordon, Waite Hoyt, Tony Lazzeri, Herb Pennock, Red Ruffing and Babe Ruth.

Above Right: CHARLES "CHINO" SMITH, 1929–1930, CENTER FIELDER—Smith had played with the Brooklyn Royal Giants in 1925–1927, hitting over .325 each season. He was nicknamed "Chino" because of his slanted eyes. The left-handed, line-drive, spray hitter hit two home runs and a triple in the first game played by black teams in Yankee Stadium. In his first year with the Lincoln club, he led the league in homers with 23. He batted over .400 twice in his brief career. The scrappy five-and-a-half-foot star's soaring career was prematurely halted when he died at 28 from a viral infection.

Left: DARLTIE "DOLLY" COOPER, 1926, PITCHER—Played only one season with the Lincoln Giants. Although he was a talented pitcher, reports hold that managers had trouble keeping Cooper in shape, which resulted in him switching teams often. During his career, 1923–1940, Cooper played for 10 different Negro Leagues teams, never playing for more than three consecutive seasons for one team.

FIRST GAME AT YANKEE STADIUM—On July 5, 1930, the Lincoln Giants became the first black professional baseball team to play in Yankee Stadium, against the Baltimore Black Sox. The Giants' strength up the middle, from left to right: Julio Rojo (catcher), Red Ryan (pitcher), Rev Cannady (second baseman) and John Beckwith (shortstop and slugger extraordinaire). Yankees owner Colonel Jacob Ruppert had opened the "House" as a supporter for the Brotherhood of Sleeping Car Porters, a labor union led by A. Philip Randolph and Milton P. Webster, that organized African American employees of the Pullman Company in August 1925.

"Let's Fill the Yankee Stadium!"

THE PULLMAN PORTERS AGAIN

2 BIG BALL GAMES!

A Double-Header—the Clash of the Season

NEW YORK   BALTIMORE

LINCOLN GIANTS vs. BLACK SOX

Saturday, July 5th

FIRST GAME AT 1:30 P.M.

Positively the Biggest Event of the Year — For
First Time in History the Famous

YANKEE STADIUM

Is Donated to the Colored People of Harlem for the Benefit of the
Brotherhood of Sleeping Car Porters by Courtesy of

COLONEL JACOB RUPPERT

OWNER OF THE NEW YORK YANKEES

BETWEEN THE GAMES

100-Yard, Special Invitation.   Half Mile, Special Invitation
Novelty Race

100,000 HARLEMITES   100,000 HARLEMITES

CAN, WILL, SHOULD, MUST, BE THERE
CONTINUOUS MUSIC BY FAMOUS BAND

GENERAL ADMISSION:

Grand Stand, $1.00   Reserved and Box Seats, $1.50

TICKETS ON SALE AT:

The Brotherhood of Sleeping Car Porters Headquarters,
139 West 136th Street

Johnnie Jackson's Restaurant .... 2289 Seventh Avenue
Amsterdam News .... 2293 Seventh Avenue
The Age .... 230 West 135th Street
Al Smith's Billiard Room .... 145th Street and 7th Avenue

"Let's Fill the Yankee Stadium"

Promotional ad for support of the Pullman Porters. The Giants defeated the Black Sox in game one, 13–4, and lost the second game, 5–3.

♦ 6 ♦

New York Black Yankees, 1932–1950

When the Lincoln Giants folded in 1930, their star, "Pop" Lloyd, managed an interim New York team, the Harlem Stars (owned by dancer Bill "Bojangles" Robinson), for the 1931 season. The next season, the Harlem club evolved into the Black Yankees, financed by Arthur Barnes and James "Soldier Boy" Semler, a tailor by trade. Semler had acquired his military moniker as a mess cook for a unit in the south of France in 1917. As league secretary, he had a reputation for unprofessional behavior in board meetings, prompting the *Chicago Defender* to call Semler's team "the stormy petrels [seabird] of Negro Baseball."

The Black Yankees also called Paterson, New Jersey, home from 1933 to 1937. The 1938 season saw the Black Yankees testing their fate at New York's Downing Stadium on Randall's Island. Paterson's strong fan support promoted the return of the Black Yankees to Paterson's Hinchliffe Stadium from 1939 to 1947. When attendance started to fall, Semler approached the president of the Rochester Redwings of the International League about renting their park for the 1948 season. The Redwings offered more playing dates and inclusion in their publicity. In essence, the Black Yankees became the only black team in the Rochester-Buffalo-Syracuse area.

The sparse and scattered black population of the area failed to support the team, forcing the franchise to leave league play to partake in independent baseball in 1949 and 1950.

The Black Yankees had offices at:

65 West 135th St., New York, NY
36 West 138th St., New York, NY
824 St. Nicholas Avenue, New York, NY
111–17 178th St., St. Albans, Queens, NY (Semler's home)
75 W. 135th St., New York, NY
67 West 135th St., New York, NY

Future Major Leaguers and Their Major League Debut Dates

Satchel Paige	Cleveland Indians	July 9, 1948
Luis Marquez	Boston Braves	April 18, 1951
George Crowe	Boston Braves	April 16, 1952

Hall of Famers, Years with Team	*Halls of Fame and Induction Years*
Satchel Paige, 1941	United States 1972, Puerto Rico 1996
Luis "Angel" Marquez, 1945	Puerto Rico 1991
George "Mule" Suttles, 1941	United States 2006
Willie "The Devil" Wells, 1945, 1946	United States 1997

Standings

Negro National League

Year	W/L	Place, Games Behind First
1936	7–14	last place
1937	11–17	incomplete findings
1938	4–17	incomplete findings
1939	15–21	5th place, 17½
1940	10–22	last place, 13½
1941	12–18	5th place, 7
1942	7–20	last place, 17½
1943	2–21	6th place, 20½
1944	4–28	last place, 19
1945	7–26	last place, 19
1946	8–40	last place, 31½
1947	10–40	last place, 27
1948	8–39	last place, 21½

Home Fields

Hinchliffe Stadium, Redwood Avenue, Walnut Street, Spruce Street and Liberty Street in Paterson, New Jersey. Seating capacity: 10,000. Played there in 1933–1937, 1939–1947.

John J. Downing Stadium, a.k.a. Triborough's Stadium, on Randall's Island, near the Triborough Bridge, between the East and Harlem Rivers, near Little Hell Gate. First game was played on July 24, 1938. Seating capacity: 22,000. Played there in 1938.

Red Wing Stadium, 500 Norton Street, Clinton Avenue, Joseph Avenue and Bastian Street in Rochester, New York. Seating capacity: 13,000. Played there in 1948.

The Black Yankees also played some home games at Dexter Park in Queens and Offermann Stadium in Buffalo, New York.

J. J. Johnson, *President*
Madison Bell, *Vice President*
Maude Semler, *Treasurer*
James Semler, *Business Manager*

James Semler, *President*
Madison Bell, *Vice President*
Jack Austin, *Manager*
Jock Waters, *Secretary*

NEW YORK BLACK YANKEES, Inc.
a n d
THE ALL NATIONS
75 WEST 135th STREET
NEW YORK CITY

Phone: Tillinghast 5-9771

Letterhead stationery

NATIONAL NEGRO LEAGUE
✦ BASEBALL ✦
DYCKMAN OVAL, 204TH STREET & NAGEL AVENUE
DOUBLE-HEADER
SUNDAY, MAY 16th
FIRST GAME STARTS 2:00 P.M.
New York Black Yanks
—VS.—
ED. BOLDEN'S
Philadelphia Stars
BLEACHERS, 30c   GRANDSTAND, 55c   BOX SEATS, 85c
Including Tax
Eighth Ave. Subway; I. R. T. Broadway Train

In 1937, before roughly 8,000 fans at Dyckman Oval, the Black Yankees took the twin-bill from the Philadelphia Stars, 10–9 and 5–2 (in seven innings).

Born Luther Robinson in Richmond, Virginia, Bill "Bojangles" Robinson was best known as a tap dancer and movie star. Besides making Shirley Temple famous, he was co-owner of the Black Yankees. Robinson is shown here dancing with Satchel Paige's first wife, Janet Howard, at their wedding in Pittsburgh.

C. THOMAS, C. JENKINS, C. SPEARMAN
Three Shining Lights in Colored Baseball.

THE ONLY PUBLICATION OF ITS KIND IN THE WORLD

FIRST EDITION—*Colored Baseball & Sports Monthly* showcased the Yankees' outfielders, Clint Thomas, Clarence "Fats" Jenkins and Clyde Spearman. You put Thomas in center, "Fats" in left and Spearman in right field, and you had one of the fleetest outfields in black baseball. Despite excellent sports coverage and provocative editorials, the "only publication of its kind" folded after two issues.

GEORGE DANIEL CROWE, 1947–1948, FIRST BASEMAN—Crowe played Major League baseball for ten years with the Cincinnati Reds (in uniform), Milwaukee Braves and St. Louis Cardinals. At one time, he held the record for the most pinch-hit home runs in the Majors with 14. His brother is Hall of Fame basketball coach Ray Crowe, who was the head coach of the Crispus Attucks High School teams that won two consecutive Indiana State titles in 1954-55 and 1955-56, led by Oscar Robertson. Big George, in 1947, played basketball for the integrated Los Angeles Red Devils, a team that also included future Brooklyn Dodger Jackie Robinson.

RICHARD WILLIAM "DICKIE" SEAY, 1940–1942, 1946–1947, SECOND BASEMAN—Seay was the only member of the 1937 Newark Eagles' Million Dollar infield of Ray Dandridge, Willie Wells and Mule Suttles who was not elected to the National Baseball Hall of Fame. An outstanding defensive middle fielder, with superb bunting and hit-and-run abilities, he was generally a light hitter. Seay appeared in three East-West All-Star Games and retired after the 1947 season as a Black Yankees icon.

LARRY "IRON MAN" BROWN, 1932, CATCHER—When it comes to Negro Leagues catchers, none was better. He earned the nickname "Iron Man" by catching 234 games in 1930. Brown was an excellent handler of pitchers and foul balls, and had a strong and accurate arm that was lethal for base stealers. Stories have it that Brown once went five years without allowing a passed ball. Brown, who played in six East-West All-Star Games, had a 31-year career in the Negro Leagues.

GEORGE LOUIS "TUBBY" SCALES, 1932–1934, 1936, 1939, 1945, SECOND BASEMAN—A consistent .300 hitter over a 25-year career, he had the ability to play several positions. Buck Leonard claimed that Scales was the best curveball hitter he ever saw. Scales also managed for 12 seasons in the Puerto Rican winter league, winning six pennants, and led the Cangrejeros de Santurce to the Caribbean World Series title in 1951. The series is the highest baseball tournament at club level in Latin America, featuring the champions from Cuba, Dominican Republic, Mexico, Puerto Rico, and Venezuela.

Opposite, bottom: 1939 BLACK YANKEES—From left to right: (front row) fourth from left, Barney Brown, Goose Curry, unknown, unknown, Zollie Wright and Terris McDuffie; (top row) unknown, Clarence "Spoony" Palm, unknown, unknown, Rev Cannady, unknown, George Scales, unknown. This team would finish in fifth place.

1933 BLACK YANKEES—From left to right: (front row) Jess Hubbard, Ted Trent, Willie Burns, Henry McHenry and Unknown; (top row) Clint Thomas, Tex Burnett, Robert Clarke, Crush Holloway, Unknown, Rev Cannady and George Scales. Burnett later became manager of the 1945 Pittsburgh Crawfords in Branch Rickey's United States League.

JOSHUA "BRUTE" JOHNSON, 1942, 1948, CATCHER—Josh Johnson backed up Josh Gibson when he played for the Homestead Grays. It was the only time in his life he was number two. Outside of baseball, he earned bachelor's (Cheyney State, 1940) and master's (Penn State, 1941) degrees. The former school superintendent is a member of the Cheyney Athletic Hall of Fame and the Springfield (IL) Sports Hall of Fame. Johnson is shown here in a Cincinnati Tigers uniform.

DOUBLE TEAMS, DOUBLE HEADER—Pitcher Jesse "Mountain Man" Hubbard, with the future "Yankee Clipper," Joe DiMaggio, James "Soldier Boy" Semler, and catcher Raleigh "Biz" Mackey. In 1932, Hubbard joined the Black Yankees and remained with the club until 1936, his final season. DiMaggio is sporting a New York cap as he goes into his rookie year, 1936, with the Yankees, after recuperating from a car accident. He had begun his professional career with the San Francisco Seals of the Pacific Coast League in 1932. Semler, along with "Bojangles" Robinson, owned the club. Mackey represented the Washington Elite Giants in the doubleheader played at Yankee Stadium.

LET'S GET IT ON!—Eight years before the color line was erased, Lester Rodney of the *NY Daily Worker* wrote a 1937 article entitled, "Paige Ask Test for Negro Stars." Paige, often portrayed as a political satirist, challenged the naysayers, "Let the winners of the World Series play [the Negro League All-Stars] just one game at Yankee Stadium, and if we don't beat them before a packed house they don't have to pay us." Paige is shown here with Hall of Famers "Big" Ed Walsh, Grover "Old Pete" Alexander, and Mayor Fiorello La Guardia on May 11, 1941. Nicknamed "The Little Flower" (he stood 5'2"), La Guardia is fondly remembered for reading comic strips over the radio to New York's children during a citywide newspaper strike.

LEROY ROBERT "SATCHEL" PAIGE, 1941, 1943, PITCHER—Paige only pitched a few games in Yankees pinstripes. In an article published by the *New York Daily Worker* on September 13, 1937, Joe DiMaggio told sportswriter Lester Rodney that *"Satchel Paige is the greatest pitcher I ever batted against."* The future Yankee Clipper was recalling those dark days in the batter's box when he faced Paige in the West Coast league during the off-season.

SATCHEL PAIGE ENTERTAINS—At the piano, Paige tickles the ivories with two team-mates, standing, along with his manager, Fred "Tex" Burnett, seated, enjoying the melodies.

SATCH'S DAY—Members of the 1971 Veterans Committee are shown with their first Negro Leagues selectee, Satchel Paige. From left to right (seated) Joe Reichler (assistant to Commissioner Bowie Kuhn), Frank Forbes and Eddie Gottlieb (booking agents), and Roy Campanella (Hall of Fame catcher); (standing) Wendell Smith (writer), Judy Johnson (Hall of Fame third baseman), Satchel Paige, Sam Lacy (writer) and Monte Irvin (Hall of Fame outfielder). Forbes was a former umpire, team owner and business manager. In his younger days, he played guard for the New York Rens basketball team. And lastly, Forbes was one of the judges at the 1947 Jersey Joe Walcott vs. Joe Louis fight at Madison Square Garden. Courtesy Sam Lacy.

GEORGE "MULE" SUTTLES, 1941, FIRST BASEMAN—The future Hall of Famer, and one of the game's most feared hitters, joined the 1937 Newark Eagles and became a part of the celebrated "million dollar infield." Spending only one season with the Black Yankees, he returned to manage his former team, the Newark Eagles, in 1942. Suttles manned the helm until 1944, with a final hurrah to baseball in 1946, managing the semi-pro Newark Buffaloes.

GOLD GLOVER ON FIRST?—No, but one of the Negro Leagues' most powerful hitters was George Suttles, from Brocton, Alabama. Here he anchors first base in Dexter Park during a 1939 contest. Suttles played in five East-West All-Star Games, hitting a monstrous .412 with a slugging percentage of .941, the highest in All-Star history.

JONATHAN CLYDE "DUDE" PARRIS, 1946–1948, FIRST BASEMAN—Parris played Negro Leagues ball with the Louisville Buckeyes, Philadelphia Stars and Baltimore Elite Giants. The Panamanian native also played in the Brooklyn Dodgers' minor league system with Class-A Elmira and was named MVP of the Eastern League. The next season, 1956, Parris won the batting title, hitting .321, with the Triple A Montreal Royals. In five seasons with Montreal, Parris's slugging percentage never fell below .400.

ALEXANDER "SLATS" NEWKIRK, 1946–1948, PITCHER—The lanky right-hander from Bridgeport, Connecticut, was not an overpowering pitcher, but had an effective slider, fastball and curve. During the 1948 season, Newkirk joined the N.Y. Cubans and finished his Negro Leagues career with the Yanks in 1949. He closed out his career with two seasons in the Provincial League with the St. Jean Braves and the Granby Red Sox in Quebec, Canada.

WALTER LEE HARDY, 1944–1948, SEC-
OND BASEMAN, SHORTSTOP—He was a
flashy infielder who generated excitement
with the fans. After five years with the Black
Yankees, Hardy joined the N.Y. Cubans for
one season. In 1950, he played briefly with the
Kansas City Monarchs, before finishing up
his career in the Provincial League with the
St. Jean Braves of Quebec in 1950 and 1951,
with a return stint with the Braves in 1955.

Above Right: WILLIE JAMES "THE DEVIL" WELLS, SR., 1945–1946, SHORT-
STOP—Tigers Hall of Fame second baseman Charlie Gehringer called him "the kind
of player you always wanted on your team, he played the way all great players play—
with everything he had." Cool Papa Bell added, "The shortstops I've seen, Wells could
cover ground better than any of them. Willie Wells was the greatest shortstop in the
world." Wells played in Mexico in 1940 and 1941, where he said that he experienced
democracy, acceptance and freedom for the first time in his life.

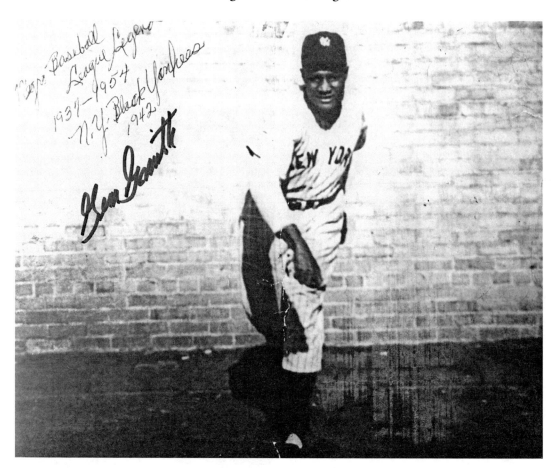

EUGENE "GENIE" SMITH, 1942, PITCHER—This was Smith's only season with the Black Yankees. The pitcher was regarded as a power thrower with a powerhouse fastball and hard-breaking slider. Earlier, in 1941, he pitched a no-hitter against the Black Yankees. Smith's 12-year career included stints with the Atlanta Black Crackers, Kansas City Monarchs, Homestead Grays, Cleveland Buckeyes and Chicago American Giants. Courtesy Wayne Stivers.

LUIS ANGEL MARQUEZ, 1945, CENTER FIELDER—Marquez, pictured in his native Aguadilla, Puerto Rico, uniform, was an outstanding center fielder for the Homestead Grays, Baltimore Elite Giants and the Cubans. In 1947, he captured the Negro National League batting title, hitting .417 and stealing 29 bases. Marquez played in four East-West All-Star Games. He had a short stay in the majors with the Boston Braves in 1951, plus stops with the Chicago Cubs and the Pittsburgh Pirates. The estrella star (superstar) was selected to the Puerto Rican Hall of Fame in 1991. Courtesy Luis Alvelo.

ROBERT SCOTT, 1946, 1950, PITCHER—Scott, who now relaxes in Macon, Georgia, recalls the facts of integration back in his day. "That wasn't reality for us. We figured, 'Hey, if Satchel [Paige] didn't go, and if Josh [Gibson] didn't go, shucks, what chance would we have of going?' Every player that played in the Negro Leagues could have played in the Major Leagues. That's just how good the players were." Scott's closest call to the majors came in 1955, when he signed with a New York Giants farm team. Courtesy Robert Scott.

MARVIN BARKER, 1936–1941, 1943–1950, OUTFIELDER, THIRD BASEMAN—Barker was manager of the Black Yankees from 1946 to 1950. One of the game's top center fielders, Barker appeared in three East-West All-Star classics, 1940, 1945 and 1948. Barker is shown here with the Philadelphia Stars in 1942, his only year in the city of brotherly love.

HENRY ALLEN "JUMBO" KIMBRO, 1941, OUTFIELDER—A mainstay and key member of the Baltimore Elite Giants for several years, he spent one season with the Black Yankees before returning to Baltimore. With a rare blend of power and speed, Kimbro possessed great range as a center fielder. A perennial All-Star, he made appearances in ten East-West games. The intense competitor closed out his career with the Birmingham Black Barons in 1952–1953. Courtesy Charles Montfort.

♦ 7 ♦

New York Cubans, 1935–1936, 1939–1950

The Latins from Manhattan, after a troubled start, became one of the most stable franchises in Negro Leagues history. In their inaugural year, they fielded one of their strongest clubs, making a unsuccessful run at the perennially tough Pittsburgh Crawfords for the title. The next season, they stumbled to the mediocre 22–23 won-lost record, six and a half games out of first place.

Owned by Alex Pompez, his Cubans lacked fan support despite their cosmopolitan composition. That problem, coupled with Pompez's impending indictment for racketeering and his flight to Mexico, meant that they did not field teams in 1937 and 1938.

Overall, in 14 seasons the New York Cubans made three playoff appearances—1935, 1941, and 1947—while capturing their lone Negro Leagues World Series title, defeating the Cleveland Buckeyes, in 1947. The franchise also left an indelible mark on white baseball as nine Cubans stars would later play in the Major Leagues.

Organized by Alex Pompez (pronounced Pom-pay)

Offices at: 84 Lenox Avenue, and 2370 Seventh Avenue (now Adam Clayton Powell, Jr., Blvd.), Manhattan, NY

Future Major Leaguers and Their Major League Debut Dates

Minnie Minoso	Cleveland Indians	April 19, 1949
Ray Noble	New York Giants	April 18, 1951
Hector Rodriquez	Chicago White Sox	April 15, 1952
George Crowe	Boston Braves	April 16, 1952
Quincy Trouppe	Cleveland Indians	April 30, 1952
Sandy Amoros	Brooklyn Dodgers	August 22, 1952
Jose Santiago	Cleveland Indians	April 17, 1954
Lino Donoso	Pittsburgh Pirates	June 18, 1955
Pat Scantlebury	Cincinnati Reds	April 19, 1956

Hall of Famers, Years with Team	*Halls of Fame and Induction Years*
Luis Arango, 1935–1939	Cuba 1986
Sandy Amoros, 1950	Cuba 1978
Bernardo Baro, 1916, 1922–1930	Cuba 1945
Ramon Bragana, 1928, 1930, 1935	Cuba 1960, Mexico 1964
Pancho Coimbre, 1940–1941, 1943–1944, 1946	Puerto Rico 1991
Marceline Correa, 1935–1936	Cuba 1986

Hall of Famers, Years with Team	Halls of Fame and Induction Years
Alejandro "Home Run" Crespo, 1940, 1946	Cuba 1973
Ray Dandridge, 1949	United States 1987, Mexico 1989
Martin Dihigo, 1935–1936, 1945	Cuba 1951, Mexico 1964, United States 1977
Lino Donoso, 1947–1949	Mexico 1988
Jose Maria Fernandez, 1935–1950	Cuba 1965
Jose "Tito" Figueroa, 1940	Puerto Rico 1992
Manuel "Cocaina" Garcia, 1935–1956	Cuba 1969, Puerto Rico 1993
Silvio Garcia, 1946–1947	Cuba 1975
Hiram Gonzales, 1950	Mexico 1993
Juan Guilbe, 1940	Puerto Rico 1992
Cando Lopez, 1935	Cuba 1984
Minnie Minoso, 1945–1948	Cuba 1983, Mexico 1994
Ray Noble, 1945–1948	Cuba 1985
Alejandro Oms, 1935	Cuba 1944
Pedro Pages, 1939, 1947	Cuba, 1997
Alex Pompez, owner	Cuba 1997, United States 2006
Hector Rodriquez, 1939, 1944	Cuba 1974
Lazaro Salazar, 1935–1936	Cuba 1959, Mexico 1964
Carlos Santiago, 1947–1948	Puerto Rico 1993
Luis Tiant, Sr., 1935–1936, 1939–1940, 1943, 1945–1947	Cuba 1965
Tetelo Vargas, 1941–1944	Puerto Rico 1992

Standings

Negro National League

Year	W/L	Place, Games Behind First
1935	30–23	2nd place, 8½
1936	22–23	3rd place, 6½
1937–1938	Did not field a team	
1939	5–22	last place, 18
1940	12–19	4th place, 11
1941	11–12	4th place, 4½
1942	8–19	5th place, 16½
1943	20–9	2nd place, 5½
1944	18–16	4th place, 6
1945	6–20	5th place, 16½
1946	28–21	2nd place, 12
1947	42–18	1st place—World Champions, defeated the Cleveland Buckeyes
1948	16–27	5th place, 16½

Negro American League

Year	W/L	Place, Games Behind First
1949	26–20	2nd place, 11½
1950	18–16	3rd place, 3½

Home Fields

Catholic Protectory Oval in the Bronx at East Tremont Avenue & Unionport Road, in the Parkchester section of the East Bronx. Seating capacity: 12,000. 1935–1936

Dyckman Oval, bounded by Nagel Avenue (NW), Academy Street (SW), Tenth Street (SE), and West 204th Street (NE), Henry Hudson Parkway and Dyckman Street. Located near Harlem Ship Canal in the Inwood section of Manhattan, near the northern tip of the island. Seating capacity: 10,000.

The Polo Grounds V, stood on Manhattan's East 159th Street, between Coogan's Bluff and the Harlem River. Built in 1911 by New York Giants owner John T. Brush, it was the city's first concrete-and-steel park. Seating capacity about 56,000 in 1935–1936; 51,856 in 1939; 56,000 in 1940–1946; 54,500 in 1947–1950.

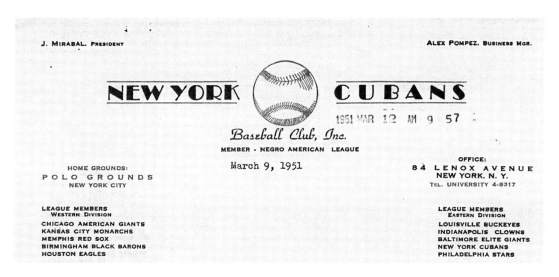

Top: New York Cubans letterhead. *Bottom:* Dyckman Oval.

MAX AND ALEX—Max Rosner (left) was owner of the very tough semipro Brooklyn Bushwicks, who gave every team, black or white, strong competition. Shown on the right is Alex Pompez, owner of the Cuban Stars. When booking agent Nat Strong suddenly died, in 1935, of a heart attack at age 61, Max Rosner and William Leuschner took over the Nat Strong Enterprise, Inc., maintaining the monopoly on booking baseball business in the city for the New York Cubans and other afro-teams. This photograph was taken in July of 1951.

GEORGE HERMAN "BABE" RUTH—Overweight and over 40, the great Bambino made his last appearance as an active player with a semipro team of "All Stars" against the N.Y. Cubans on September 29, 1935. The game was played at Dyckman Oval, with Ruth guarding first base. Ruth connected for a long double and begged a walk in five plate appearances. He handled 12 chances at first base without a miscue. Ruth's team of has-beens was defeated by the Cubans and Luis Tiant, Sr., 6–1.

PATRICIO ATHELSTAN "PAT" SCANTLEBURY, 1944–1950, PITCHER—After several productive years in the Negro Leagues, Scantlebury joined the Cincinnati Reds at the age of 38 for one season, 1956. That year, in six appearances, he gave up 14 runs in 19 innings of pitching. Earlier, in 1947, he pitched in two games of the Negro World Series against the Cleveland Buckeyes, picking up a victory as the Cubans defeated the Buckeyes five games to one. The lefty was known for his assortment of curves, sliders and screwballs. Scantlebury also pitched in the 1946, 1949 and 1950 East-West All-Star Games.

HECTOR ANTONIO RODRIGUEZ, 1944, THIRD BASEMAN—Sometimes confused with second baseman Arturo Antonio "El Pollo" Rodríguez, this Rodriguez played 11 years in the Mexican League, with several teams. In 1951, Rodríguez was acquired by the Brooklyn Dodgers from the Tuneros de San Luis Potosí of the Mexican League. He was assigned to Brooklyn's farm club, the Montreal Royals (pictured), where he batted .302. That year, on December 6, he was traded by the Dodgers to the Chicago White Sox. Rodriguez became the White Sox's regular third baseman in 1952, appearing in 124 games. It would be his only season in major league baseball.

GUILLERMO VARGAS, 1949, OUTFIELDER—According to the Howe News Bureau, in his only season with the Cubans, he hit .278 in 36 games. Vargas had 35 hits in 126 at-bats, with six doubles and two triples, for a .357 slugging percentage. The following season, he played with Nuevo Laredo Tecolotes in the Mexican League. In 1952, he played with the Drummonville Cubs of the Canadian Provincial League, where he hit .282 and slugged .363.

RAUL LOPEZ, 1948–1950, PITCHER—When the Cubans moved to the Negro American League, Howe News Bureau captured his performance on the mound for the 1949 and 1950 seasons. In 15 games, he pitched 93 innings, gave up 85 hits, and struck out 85 batters, with an ERA of 3.48. Lopez's won-lost record was 5–4. As a product of the New York Giants, he played the next two season in AAA with the Jersey City Giants and the Ottawa Giants, and later joined the Oakland Oaks of the PCL.

VICTOR "SLICKER" GREENIDGE, 1941–1944, PITCHER—The Panamanian native started his career with the Cubans touted as one of the best rookie pitchers. He had modest success during this four-year stay in the Negro Leagues. He was a member of the Almendares Scorpions team that won the Cuban Winter League championship in 1943-1944.

JOSE MARIA "PEPE" FERNANDEZ, JR., 1948–1950, CATCHER—The son of Jose Senior, he inherited his father's tools behind the plate. Pepe saw limited action during the last years of the Negro Leagues. He was the nephew of Rodolfo Fernandez.

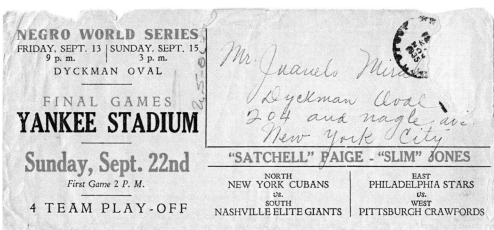

Top: FERNANDO "EL BICHO" DIAZ, 1945–1950, SECOND BASE AND SHORT-STOP—Quicker than a gnat, the rangy "Bicho" could play all the infield positions. "Bicho" is Spanish for insect. Diaz was one of the quickest players on the team. An average hitter, according to the Howe News Bureau, he had 634 at-bats over four seasons, a batting average of .246, and slugging percentage of .334, with 29 doubles and nine triples. The Cuban star returned to his homeland to play out his career with the Marianao, Habana, and Almendares teams until the winter of 1956-1957.

Bottom: FOUR TEAMS, TWO GAMES, ONE DAY—A common attraction in the Negro Leagues was to have four teams in a playoff round-robin tournament. One of the most highly advertised games was the matchup between Leroy "Satchell" [sic] Paige and Stuart "Slim" Jones. This promotional envelope was sent in November 1935 to Juanelo Marabal, a pitcher for the New York Cubans.

LUIS ELEUTERIO TIANT, SR., 1935–1936, 1939–1940, 1943, 1945–1947, PITCHER—
The father of Boston Red Sox great Luis Tiant, Jr., Senor Tiant pitched in the 1935 and
1947 East-West All-Star Games. In the championship season, "Sir Skinny" won ten
games (with three shutouts) against no losses. Tiant started two World Series games
against the Buckeyes. Tiant was known for his array of junk pitches and an undetectable
pick-off motion. Tiant became a member of the Cuban Hall of Fame in 1965.

MARTIN DIHIGO, 1935–36, 1945, MANAGER, OUTFIELDER—*"He was just a great natural athlete,"* Monte Irvin recalled (*Elysian Fields Quarterly* 18, no. 2, 2001, "Martin Dihigo"). *"He could run like a deer and had a great arm. He played the infield and the outfield, and he was a great pitcher. In Cuba they regarded him as the finest of all Cuban players and they had major leaguers like Mike Gonzalez, Dolf Luque and others. Gonzalez and Luque had dark complexions, but they weren't black, so they could play organized ball. Anybody could play except a Negro. Some of the blacks would adopt Latin names in hopes of getting into the majors."*

SCHOOLBOY TAYLOR—A native of Hartford, Connecticut, John Taylor (right, seen with Satchel Paige) was only 21 when he no-hit Satchel Paige's Trujillo All-Stars before 22,500 fans at the Polo Grounds. In this September 23, 1937, contest, Taylor only allowed two balls to be hit out of the infield, with no one reaching second base, as the New York Cubans won, 2–0. At the time, Paige's All-Stars had been promoted as "the most talented team of tan stars on the circuit."

Taylor shows off his pitching form. Courtesy Estelle Taylor.

Opposite, bottom: JOSE ANTONIO "TITO" FIGUEROA, 1940, PITCHER—The least-known athlete of these all-stars is Tito Figueroa. In 1935, the multi-talented pitcher won a Caribbean Olympic gold medal in the javelin. Later, with the Mayaguez Indians, he led the Puerto Rican League with 137 strikeouts. In his only season in the black leagues, Figueroa was the Opening Day pitcher at Yankee Stadium, where he led the Cubans over the Black Yankees, 8 to 1. After the season he returned to Puerto Rico. Figueroa was elected to the Puerto Rican Hall of Fame in 1992. Pictured, from left to right, are Andres Julio "Grillo" Baez, "Pancho" Coimbre, Juan Guilbe, Figueroa and "Rabbit" Martinez. Courtesy Luis Alvelo.

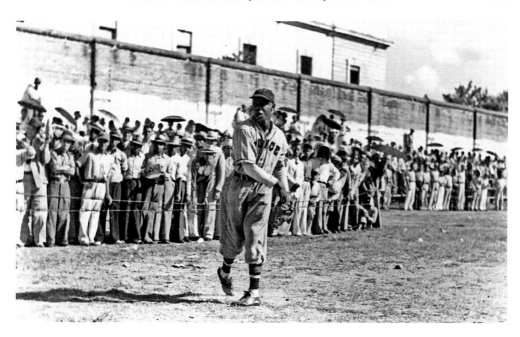

SILVIO GARCIA, 1940, 1946–1947, PITCHER, SHORTSTOP—Garcia, from Limonar, Cuba, started his career as a pitcher until he was hurt by a wicked line drive. Converting to the infield, Garcia became a fine fielder and an excellent hitter. He played in four East-West All-Star Games and was selected to the Cuban Hall of Fame in 1975. He is shown here with the Ponce Lions of 1939-1940. Courtesy Luis Alvelo.

READY FOR BATTLE—The Cubans are ready to take the field. Pictured on the far left is ace pitcher Dave Barnhill. Fifth from the left is future Puerto Rican Hall of Famer Pancho Coimbre.

Opposite: FRANCISCO "PANCHO" COIMBRE, 1940–1946, OUTFIELDER—Called by baseball historian Todd Bolton the greatest Puerto Rican player ever to play in the Negro Leagues, he appeared in two East-West All-Star Games. Some Islanders consider Coimbre even better than Roberto Clemente. In the Winter Leagues, Clemente hit for a career .323 average, while Coimbre hit .337. In 13 seasons with the Ponce Lions, Pancho struck out only 29 times in 1,915 at-bats. Coimbre later scouted for the Pittsburgh Pirates. In 1989, he died in a house fire. On May 21, 1992, through the efforts of historian Luis Alvelo and others, the Francisco "Pancho" Coimbre Museum was dedicated in Ponce. Coimbre was a charter member of the 1991 Puerto Rican Hall of Fame. Courtesy Luis Alvelo.

Top and above: THE GUILBE BROTHERS—From left to right: Felix "Felo," Juan "Telo," and Jesus. Felix played for the Baltimore Elite Giants from 1946 to 1947, while Juan starred at first base and pitched for the 1940 Cubans. The youngest Guilbe, Jesus, never made it to the Negro Leagues. Juan is considered by some historians the best center fielder in Puerto Rican baseball. Kneeling below are Jesus, Juan and Felix, the best brother trio in baseball until the Alou brothers, Felipe, Matty, and Jesus, came along. Courtesy Luis Alvelo.

CLARO DUANY, 1944, 1947, OUT-FIELDER—The left-handed power hitter always hit for a high average. Between seasons with the N.Y. Cubans, he hit .375 and .364 with Monterrey in the Mexican League. He returned to the club in 1947 to help them win the Negro League World Championship. Pictured here with Marianao in 1944–1945, he led the winter league with a .340 batting average. Courtesy Luis Alvelo.

PEDRO ARMANDO "GAMO" PAGES, 1939, 1947, CENTER FIELDER—Shown here in 1947, Pages was known for his speed on the base paths and his excellent eye at the plate. Batting in the tough second spot of the batting order, he hit around .300 most seasons. Pedro Pages (pronounced "Pah-hez") was elected to the Cuban Hall of Fame in 1997. The native of Matanzas closed out his career in 1951 with Sherbrooke of the Canadian Provincial League, hitting .244. Courtesy Todd Bolton.

PAGES AND GARCIA—Pedro Pages barely beats pitcher Manuel "Cocaina" Garcia on a close play at first base. The left-handed Garcia had a big roundhouse curve, a Niagara Falls sinker, and a fastball described by some as "like lightning." Garcia played for the Cubans in 1935 and 1936. He was later elected to the Cuban Hall of Fame in 1969 and the Puerto Rican Hall of Fame in 1993. Courtesy Luis Alvelo.

Right: FELIX RAFAEL DELGADO, 1941, OUTFIELDER AND FIRST BASE-MAN—Delgado only played one season with the Cubans as a part-time outfielder and first baseman. He also played for the Cuban Stars back in 1936. Delgado is pictured here in his San Juan uniform. Courtesy Wayne Stivers.

Below: DAVE "IMPO" BARNHILL, 1941–1949, PITCHER—Barnhill (right) was the ace of the Cubans' pitching staff in the 1940s. He was called "Impo" for his smallish stature. A master of defense at his position, he was waterbug quick off the mound. Despite his minuscule appearance, Barnhill's bullish physicality was apparent to all batters. With a procrastinating curve, sympathy card slider and a funny bone fastball, batters found him harder to solve than a Walter Mosley mystery. At left is battery mate Roy Campanella, as they prepared for the 1942 East-West All-Star game.

JAMES "PEE WEE" JENKINS, 1946–1950, PITCHER—Jenkins also pitched for the Indianapolis Clowns and the Birmingham Black Barons. Small in stature, Jenkins had to rely on a wide variety of pitches that he commanded with superb control. Jenkins also played with Three Rivers in the Provincial League, and later with Winnipeg in the Mandak League. He retired in 1953 with the Brandon club (Mandak) after a 5–2 won-lost record. Courtesy Wayne Stivers.

JOSE GUILLERMO "PANTS" SANTIAGO, 1947–1948, PITCHER—The Puerto Rican right-hander, from Coamo, started his professional career with the Cubans in 1947. He would later pitch for the Cleveland Indians in 1954 and 1955, and also the Kansas City A's in 1956. Santiago was elected to the Puerto Rican Baseball Hall of Fame in 1993.

LET'S GIVE THE UMPIRE SOME LOVE—Shown here in 1941, the Cubans, led by finger-pointing manager Jose Fernandez, Sr., tease umpire Bill Harris.

LORENZO "CHIQUITIN" CABRERA, 1947–1950, FIRST BASEMAN—The "golpeador pesado" (heavy hitter) hit .352 in leading the Cubans to the 1947 world championship. The Cienfuegos native hit .333 and .377 the next two seasons. He finished his career in the 1950s with various minor league teams that included Oakland (PCL), Ottawa (IL), and Del Rio (Big State League), with his last hurrah, in 1956, with Tijuana-Nogales of the Arizona-Mexican League. Courtesy Luis Alvelo.

1947 WORLD CHAMPIONS IN THE POLO GROUNDS—The New York Cubans, from left to right: (front row) Lino Donoso, Rabbit Martinez, Jose Santiago, Chiflan Clark, Pee Wee Jenkins, Luis Tiant, Sr.; (middle row) Louis Louden, Minnie Minoso, Pedro Pages, Martin Crue, Dave Barnhill and Silvio Garcia; (top row) trainer Pedro Ulacia, Homero Ariosa, Pat Scantlebury, Lorenzo Cabrera, Ray Noble, Jose Fernandez, Sr., Pedro Diaz, Barney Morris and Claro Duany. They defeated the Cleveland Buckeyes, four games to one.

LINO DONOSO, 1947–1949, PITCHER—After leaving the Cubans, Donoso spent the next four seasons with Veracruz Aguila in the Mexican League. As a native of Cuba, Donoso had great success in Mexico, resulting in his election to their Hall of Fame in 1988. He would later play for the Pittsburgh Pirates in 1955 and 1956, compiling a 4–6 won-lost record.

RAFAEL MIGUEL "RAY" NOBLE, 1945–1948, CATCHER—From Central Hatillo, the Cuban catcher was well known for his powerful arm and for being a splendid receiver. A solid hitter with power, he batted over .325 for the 1947 championship team. Noble later signed with the New York Giants organization and played with the Jersey City Giants in the International League (1949) and the Oakland Oaks in the Pacific Coast League (1950), before joining the parent club in 1951, where he spent three intermittent seasons.

HORACIO "RABBIT" MARTINEZ, 1935–1936, 1939–1947, SHORTSTOP—Rabbit flashes the colors of the Tigres del Licey team based in Santo Domingo, D.R. Martinez made five East-West All-Star Game appearances, in 1940, 1941, 1943, 1944 and 1945 for the Cubans, the most of any Latin American player. Courtesy Luis Alvelo.

Opposite, bottom: MINNIE—Minoso was also "corredor rapido" (speedy). When he joined the majors, he led the American League in stolen bases three consecutive seasons, 1951–1953. He also led the AL in triples three times. Minoso played in major league All-Star Games in 1951–1954, 1957, and 1959–1960. An excellent hitter, he led the American League in total bases in 1954 with 304. Minoso was also a standout in left field, winning Gold Glove Awards in 1957, 1959, and 1960. He was voted Rookie of the Year in 1945-46, playing for Marianao in the Cuban Winter League. Courtesy The Rucker Archive.

SATURNINO ORESTES ARRIETA "MIN-
NIE" MINOSO, 1946–1948, THIRD BASE-
MAN—Minoso was the El Jugador mas de
Valor (MVP) of any league he played in. If one
were to combine all his hits from the major
leagues, Negro Leagues, Cuban Leagues and
Mexican Leagues, Minoso would have close to
4,000 hits. In 1953, Minoso with Marianao
was voted "Outstanding Player" by the Cuban
writers, beating outfielder Pedro Formental of
the Havana Reds by 15 votes. Havana's *Bohe-
mia* magazine awarded $500 to Minoso. Cour-
tesy The Rucker Archive.

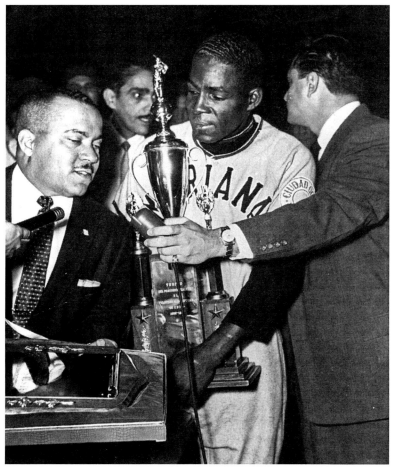

ARMANDO BERNANDO VAZQUEZ, 1948, FIRST BASEMAN—A native of Guines, Cuba, Vazquez also played for the Indianapolis Clowns and the Cubans at all the infield positions. Normally a first baseman, the smooth fielder was known for his line drives to all fields. In 1952, he teamed with rookie shortstop Hank Aaron of the Indianapolis Clowns. The happy-go-lucky athlete was the clubhouse comic everywhere he played.

Opposite, top: THE CUBAN TRIO OF 1949—Pitcher Pat Scantlebury (left), future Hall of Fame third baseman Ray Dandridge (center) and Quincy Trouppe (right). In 1948, Dandy Ray became manager of the Cubans. At age 39, Trouppe became the first African American catcher in the American League (before Elston Howard), when he joined the 1952 Cleveland Indians for six games. On May 3, when relief pitcher Sam "Toothpick" Jones entered the game, they formed the first black battery in American League history. Courtesy The Rucker Archives.

Bottom: CELEBRATION TIME—The 1949 team celebrates in the locker room, from left to right; Jose Fernandez, Sr., Pee Wee Jenkins, Jose Santiago (standing), Lorenzo Cabrera (sitting), Pedro Diaz, Pat Scantlebury and Louis Louden.

NOW WARMING UP FOR THE KANSAS CITY MONARCHS—Pitcher extraordinaire Satchel Paige warms up at Yankee Stadium on August 2, 1942, for the second game of a doubleheader between the Monarchs and the New York Cuban Stars. Paige and Hilton Smith combined to pitch a one-hitter. Before an estimated 30,000 fans, the Monarchs triumphed over the Cubans, 9–0. The Philadelphia Stars defeated Roy Campanella and his Baltimore Elite Giants in the first game, 7–4.

JUAN ESTEBAN "THE DOMINICAN DEER" VARGAS, 1941–1944, OUTFIELDER—He is sometimes confused with Jose "Huesito" Vargas, from Cuba, who played for the New York Cubans in 1939 and 1940. This Santo Domingo native, during some 1947 exhibition games in San Juan, batted .500, going 7-for-14 against the visiting New York Yankees, at the age of 41. Dr. Peter Bjarkman, Latin American baseball historian, wrote, "The slender, wiry outfielder and shortstop ... is without doubt the most accomplished Dominican native never to spend a single day in the majors."

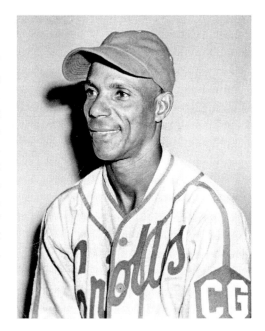

RONALD "BLAZER" TEASLEY, 1948, OUTFIELDER, FIRST BASEMAN—Teasley played one year with the Cubans club after being released by the Brooklyn Dodgers' Olean Oilers (of Olean, NY) in the Pony League. The three-time Mandak allstar is shown here in 1950 with the Carmack Cardinals. His batting average of .500 is still a record at Detroit's Wayne State University. Upon retirement from baseball, he earned a degree from Wayne State and spent 34 years with the Detroit Board of Education. In 1986, Teasley was inducted into the Wayne State University Hall of Fame.

SUGAR RAY—This undated photograph shows an unidentified New York Cubans player, boxer Sugar Ray Robinson, and Kansas City Monarchs catcher Frank Duncan. Considered one of the greatest boxers of all time, Sugar Ray Robinson held the world welterweight title from 1946 to 1951, and by 1958, he had become the first boxer to win a divisional world championship five times.

HERBERT ALBERT "RAP" DIXON, 1935, OUTFIELDER—Rap's younger brother, Paul, called him a "beautiful curve ball hitter." On July 5, 1930, Dixon was credited with being the first black player to hit a home run in Yankee Stadium. In the first inning, Dixon, with Jud Wilson on base, slammed a homer off of Bill Holland of the Lincoln Giants, into the right field bleachers. In the second game of the doubleheader, he hit two more home runs. An outstanding outfielder, Dixon died at the age of 39 in Detroit, Michigan.

RILEY STEWART, 1949–1950, PITCHER— Stewart started his career with the Memphis Red Sox (pictured) in 1946, before going to the Chicago American Giants and the Harlem Globetrotters. His last year in pro ball was with the Cubans in 1950. Stewart claimed he earned $250 a month with $6 a day for meal money. "That was real big money back in those days," said Stewart. A graduate of Leland College in Baker, Louisiana, Stewart later became principal at Bossier's Airline High School in Bossier Parish, Louisiana. Courtesy Wayne Stivers.

IN EVENT OF RAIN, GOOD ON NEXT ANNOUNCED DATE

Game   8:45 P. M.

Sept. 19, 1947   Sept. 19, 1947

UPPER
BOX SEAT

POLO GROUNDS
FRIDAY NITE, SEPT. 19, 1947

UPPER
BOX SEAT

EST. PRICE $1.67
Federal Tax   .33
TOTAL $2.00

NEGRO WORLD SERIES

EST. PRICE $1.67
Federal Tax   .33
TOTAL $2.00

SEC. 30

N. Y. CUBANS
VS
CLEVELAND BUCKEYES

SEC. 30

BOX   BOX

THIS ticket may not be resold or offered for resale at a premium in excess of 75 cents plus lawful taxes.

Above: FIRST GAME OF THE 1947 NEGRO WORLD SERIES—The Cubans met the Cleveland Buckeyes at the Polo Grounds, before roughly 5,500 fans. Unfortunately, after six innings, the game ended in a 5–5 tie. The Buckeyes took the second game at Yankee Stadium, 10–7. The Cubans went on to win the next four games, 6–0 (Cleveland's Municipal Stadium), 9–4 (Philadelphia's Shibe Park), 9–2 (Chicago's Comiskey Park), and the final game in Cleveland, 6–5.

Left: ALEJANDRO "HOME RUN" CRESPO, 1940, 1946, OUTFIELDER—The power-hitting Crespo served as the Cubans' cleanup hitter during the 1940 season and earned a trip to the East-West classic in Chicago. The next season, Crespo came to the Mexican League and batted .361/.423/.579 with 14 triples, 90 runs and 86 RBIs in 104 games for the Torreon Cotton Dealers. Overall, Crespo hit .320/.375/.485 with 565 RBIs in 712 games in the Mexican League. With several outstanding years in the Cuban Winter Leagues, he was voted into the Cuban Baseball Hall of Fame in 1973. Courtesy Charles Montfort.

FRANCISCO "CISCO KID" SOSTRE, 1947, PITCHER—After pitching for the San Juan Senators in the 1945-46 winter season, Sostre signed with the Chicago Cubs in 1946 and was optioned to the Tacoma Tigers of the Western International League. He started the 1947 season with the Cubans, before signing in July with the Samford Bombers of the Colonial League.

◆ 8 ◆

Brooklyn Eagles, 1935

The precursors to the Newark Eagles, this talented team sent four players to the 1935 East-West All-Star Game: Leon Day (pitcher), George Giles (first baseman), Fats Jenkins (left fielder) and pinch-hitter Ed Stone. The Eagles and the Newark Browns later merged into one awesome team, the Newark Eagles.

Brooklyn Eagles

Abe and Effa Manley, 741 St. Nicholas Avenue, New York, NY
Mae Williams, officer, 304 West 139th Street
Office at 2376 Seventh Avenue (now Adam Clayton Powell, Jr., Blvd.)

Hall of Famer, Years with Team	Halls of Fame and Induction Years
Leon Day, 1935	Puerto Rico 1993, United States 1995
Clarence "Fats" Jenkins, 1935	Naismith Memorial Basketball Hall of Fame, 1963
Ben Taylor, 1935	United States 2006

Standings

Negro National League

Year	W/L	Place, Games Behind First
1935	28–31	6th place, 13½

No future major league players.

Home Field

Ebbets Field, in the Pigtown section of Flatbush. Defined by Bedford Avenue (right field) (on the east side), Montgomery Street (left field) (N), Franklin Avenue (later Cedar Place, then McKeever Place) (third base) (W), and Sullivan Place (first base) (S). Seating capacity: about 28,000 in 1935.

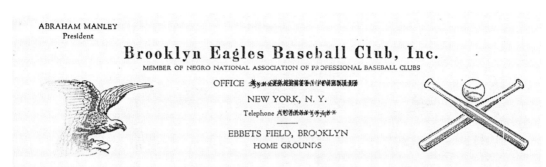

Brooklyn Eagles letterhead

ADVERTISING FOR THE NEGRO NATIONAL ASSOCIATION OF PROFESSIONAL BASEBALL CLUBS—The Brooklyn Eagles faced the Homestead Grays in a four-game series. On Saturday, the Eagles took a beating, 20–7. In the first game of the Sunday doubleheader, they were victorious, 18–9, but lost the second game, 4–2, in seven innings. The mighty Eagles evened the series by taking the final game, 4–2.

Above: BROOKLYN EAGLES, 1935—In their only year in the Negro National League, the Eagles work out in Jacksonville, Florida, to fine-tune their skills for the upcoming season. From left to right: (front row) Burnalle "Bun" Hayes, Clyde "Little Splo" Spearman, Fred "Tex" Burnett, Dennis Gilcrest, Jim "Pepper" Martin and Leon Day; (back row) Ben Taylor, S. Thompson, unknown, Lamon Yokely, Spencer Davis, George Giles, Cofield Lewis, Elbert Williams, and Ted "Double Duty" Radcliffe.

Left: RAP DIXON, 1935, OUTFIELDER—Dixon spent the first half of the season with the Eagles before joining the New York Cubans for a championship run. Herbert Albert Dixon acquired the nickname "Rap" as a member of the Steelton (PA) High School team. He had a reputation for consistently rapping out hits and home runs. With the Baltimore Black Sox, in 1929, he rapped out 14 consecutive hits in five games against the Grays and the Hilldale Club, including nine singles, four doubles and one home run.

BROOKLYN EAGLES AT EBBETS FIELD—From left to right; manager Ben Taylor, Laymon Yokely, C. B. Griffin, Roy Williams, Rap Dixon, Ted Page, George Giles, Clarence Palm, Bun Hayes, Harry Williams, Ted "Double Duty" Radcliffe, Tex Burnett, Elbert Williams, Addie Ward, Ed Stone, Dennis Gilchrist, Leon Day and Bill Yancey.

LEON DAY, 1935, PITCHER—When asked to name the best Negro Leagues pitcher, Birmingham Black Baron shortstop and .400 hitter Artie Wilson quickly cited Day. *"Yes, Leon Day was the greatest all-around baseball man I have ever seen. He could hit, run, throw, and play every single position there was. He was a great player. He could probably have caught, too. How many players do you see today that had his skills that can hit .290 or so? There are not too many of them that could pitch and hit with the same regularity that Leon Day could. And he could have beaten Satchel Paige any time he wanted to."* Day pitched a no-hitter on Opening Day in 1946, against the Philadelphia Stars.

CLARENCE REGINALD "FATS" JENKINS, 1935, LEFT FIELDER—Fats Jenkins was known for his exceptional quickness on the base paths and in the outfield. The left-handed hitter was a slap hitter and could drag a bunt with the best. After one season with the Eagles, Jenkins played for the New York Black Yankees in 1936. In 1963, Jenkins was inducted as a member of the New York Rens basketball team into the Naismith Memorial Basketball Hall of Fame.

Opposite, bottom: NEW YORK RENS—The Rens, named after the Harlem Renaissance Casino, made their debut on November 3, 1923. They defeated the Collegiate Big Five, 28–22. It was the preliminary event to the big social dance that customarily followed at the Casino. Organized by Robert L. Douglas (inset), a native of St. Kitts (British West Indies), the Rens were America's first black professional basketball team. Also, the Rens won the first world basketball championship in March of 1939, beating the National Basketball League champions, the Oshkosh All-Stars, 34–25.

Douglas was the first black man inducted into the Naismith Memorial Basketball Hall of Fame (1972), with his Rens admitted as a unit in 1963. From left to right: Clarence "Fats" Jenkins, Bill Yancey, John Holt, James "Pappy" Ricks, Eyre Saitch, Charles "Tarzan" Cooper and "Wee Willie" Smith.

FATS AND OSCAR—Fats Jenkins was an outstanding point guard for the Rens. Jenkins also played for several New York baseball teams: the Lincoln Giants (1920, 1928, 1930), Harlem Stars (1931), Black Yankees (1932–1934, 1936–1938), Brooklyn Eagles (1935) and managed the Brooklyn Royal Giants (1939–1940). Jenkins, the ultimate history maker, also played in the first East-West All-Star Game (1933) at Comiskey Park. Jenkins is shown here with future Hall of Famer Oscar Charleston (right), when they played with the Harrisburg (PA) Giants in 1925.

HIGH FLYING EAGLES—From left to right: Frank "Chink" McCoy (in last year's Newark Dodgers uniform), outfielder Crush Holloway, outfielder Clint Thomas, outfielder Ed "Black Cat" Stone, and unknown.

PULLEN, DIXON AND HOLLOWAY—O'Neal "Neal" Pullen did not play for the Brooklyn Eagles, but the catcher spent time with the 1920 Brooklyn Royal Giants and the Lincoln Giants. Herbert "Rap" Dixon, third baseman, would leave the 1935 Eagles in mid-season to join the newly formed New York Cubans for a title run against the tough Pittsburgh Crawfords. Crush Holloway, an outfielder, also played for the 1932 New York Black Yankees.

BENJAMIN HARRISON "BEN, OLD RELIABLE" TAYLOR, MANAGER—He was the Rolls-Royce of first basemen around the turn of the century and went on to Hall of Fame notoriety.

In July of 1935, Taylor announced his retirement from the Brooklyn Eagles. The *Chicago Defender* reported, "Ben Taylor, a veteran of 26 years of valuable service to Race baseball, a man who has inspired, trained and led baseball teams for many years, should not be left out of baseball. Ben has one of the keenest minds in all baseball and knows the game from all angles. I do not know of any player, past or present, who is more deserving of a place in Negro baseball than Ben Taylor."

♦ 9 ♦

Brooklyn Brown Dodgers, 1945–1946

The Brown Dodgers were members of the United States League, an experimental league created by Brooklyn Dodgers executive Branch Rickey as a developmental venue for black ball players. Joseph W. Hall was president. The U.S. League consisted, at various times, of the Atlanta Black Crackers, Chicago Brown Bombers, Detroit Motor City Giants, Philadelphia Hilldales, Pittsburgh/Montreal Crawfords, Toledo Cubs/Rays, Boston Blues, Cleveland Clippers, and Milwaukee Tigers. The league lasted two years. Its failure was due to the successful transition of Jackie Robinson and Larry Doby to the major leagues, ending decades of segregated baseball, as former Negro Leaguers gradually migrated into mainstream baseball.

Brooklyn Brown Dodgers office at 215 Montague Street, Brooklyn, NY
Michael J. Femenella, Jr., officer, 82 Robinson Avenue, Great Kills, Staten Island, NY
Helen L. Snowden, officer, 383 Warburton Avenue, Yonkers, NY
Eleanor M. Speckenbach, officer, 41–43 77th Street, Jackson Heights, NY

Hall of Famer, Year with team	*Hall of Fame and Induction Year*
Oscar Charleston, 1945	United States 1976

United States League Standings

1945	3rd place	won-lost record not available
1946	3rd place	won-lost record not available

Home Field

Ebbets Field, in the Pigtown section of Flatbush. Defined by Bedford Avenue (right field) (on the east side), Montgomery Street (left field) (N), Franklin Avenue (later Cedar Place, then McKeever Place) (third base) (W), and Sullivan Place (first base) (S). Seating capacity: about 34,000 in 1945–1946.

BRANCH RICKEY—In 1945, the shrewd promoter started the United States Baseball League to scout potential black talent for his all-white Dodgers. The charter teams were the Pittsburgh Crawfords, Toledo Cubs, Chicago Brown Bombers, Detroit Motor City Giants, Philadelphia Hilldales, and his Brooklyn Brown Dodgers. He picked African Americans Gus Greenlee and John Schackleford as his front men, naming them Vice-President and President, respectively.

OSCAR McKINLEY CHARLESTON, 1945, MANAGER—Charleston was selected by league founder Branch Rickey to manage his all-black Dodgers team. Rickey made no promises that his United States League would provide an opportunity for African Americans to integrate the majors, meanwhile criticizing the black leagues for lack of organization, saying they were in the "zone of a racket." Courtesy Dr. Alice Carter.

HERBERT "DOC" BRACKEN, 1946, PITCHER—When he played for the Cleveland Buckeyes, Bracken would pass himself off as Puerto Rican Alfredo Bragana, in hopes of playing in the major leagues. On June 4, 1946, new manager Hayward Jackson announced that the Brown Dodgers had purchased the entire St. Louis Giants baseball team in order to get the ace hurler. Jackson said owner George Armstrong had originally planned to purchase only Bracken's contract, but that Clarence Palm, St. Louis manager, countered with "the whole club will have to go with him." Courtesy Dr. Alice Carter.

STANLEY RUDOLF "DOC" GLENN, CATCHER, 1945—Glenn and Bill "Ready" Cash were the mainline catchers for several top-notch Philadelphia Stars teams during the 1940s. Glenn retired in Philadelphia and was active as president of the Negro Leagues Baseball Players Association for several years. He became a member of the Eastern Shore Baseball Hall of Fame in Maryland (2004). In 2006, Glenn published his auto-biography, *Don't Let Anyone Take Your Joy Away: An Inside Look at Negro League Base-ball and Its Legacy.* He played one season with the Brown Dodgers.

Left: ROY ALEXANDER "RED" PARNELL, OUTFIELDER, 1945—An excellent left fielder for the Philadelphia Stars from 1937 to 1943, Parnell hit for average with occasional power. In 1934, he represented the Nashville Elite Giants at the East-West All-Star Game, and he returned in 1939 for the Philadelphia Stars. Parnell played only one season with the Brown Dodgers. The native of Terrell, Texas, finished his 25-year career with the Houston Eagles in 1950. *Right:* CLARENCE "SPOONY" PALM, 1945–1946, CATCHER—A native of Clarendon, Arkansas, the much-traveled receiver also anchored the pitching staffs for the Birmingham Black Barons, Homestead Grays, Cleveland Giants, Akron Tyrites, Pittsburgh Crawfords, and Philadelphia Stars. His 20-year career also included stints in New York with the Black Yankees in 1936, 1938–1939, 1943 and 1946, and also the Brooklyn Eagles in 1935. In 1937, he caught ace Satchel Paige for Martin Dihigo's Santo Domingo Stars. Here he wears his 1939-40 San Juan uniform.

♦ 10 ♦

Brooklyn Dodgers, 1947–1957

Hall of Famers

Jackie Robinson
Roy Campanella
Sandy Amoros

Halls of Fame and Induction Years

United States 1962
United States 1969, Mexico 1972
Cuba 1978

Former Negro League Players, Team Years

Sandy Amoros, 1952, 1954–1957
Dan Bankhead, 1947, 1950–1951

Joe Black, 1952–1955
Roy Campanella, 1948–1957

Junior Gilliam, 1953–1957

Don Newcombe, 1949–1951, 1954–1957
Charlie Neal, 1956–1957
Jackie Robinson, 1947–1955

Years with Negro League Team

1950, New York Cubans
1940–42, 1944, Birmingham Black Barons
1946–1947, Memphis Red Sox
1943–1950, Baltimore Elite Giants
1937, Washington Elite Giants,
1938–1945, Baltimore Elite Giants
1945, Nashville Black Vols,
1946–1950, Baltimore Elite Giants
1944–1945, Newark Eagles
1948, Atlanta Black Crackers
1945, Kansas City Monarchs

Most Valuable Players

Jackie Robinson, 1949
Roy Campanella, 1951, 1953, 1955
Don Newcombe, 1956

Cy Young Award Winner

Don Newcombe, 1956

Rookies of the Year

Jackie Robinson, 1947
Don Newcombe, 1949
Joe Black, 1952
Jim Gilliam, 1953

Retired Numbers of Negro Leagues Players

Jim Gilliam, #19
Roy Campanella, #39
Jackie Robinson, #42

A STAR IS BORN—Robinson was born on January 31, 1919, in Cairo (pronounced KAY-ro), Georgia, on Hadley Ferry Road, a blue-collar town of about 10,000 folks. In 1997, the Cairo High School Syrupmakers renamed its baseball grounds "Jackie Robinson Field."

Opposite, top: EBBETS FIELD—Built on a garbage dump once known as "Pig Town," it opened in 1913 and was considered one of the premier parks of its time. It eventually become the smallest park, capacity wise, in the National League and was demolished in 1960. The Ebbets Field Apartments were built on the former site and opened in 1962. Ten years later, they were renamed the Jackie Robinson Apartments, the year Robinson died.

Bottom: EBBETS FIELD—The legendary home of the Brooklyn Dodgers holds many distinctions in the history of black baseball in New York. At the park on April 15, 1947, Jackie Robinson appeared in his first major league game, becoming the first African American to play in the major leagues in the twentieth century. It was also at Ebbets Field on August 26, 1947, that Brooklyn Dodger Dan Bankhead became the first African American to pitch in the major leagues when he was brought in as a relief pitcher.

WORLD PEACE!—After the end of the 1945 season, Jackie Robinson was summoned to the Brooklyn Dodgers' office under the guise of playing the following season for the Brooklyn Brown Dodgers of the United States League. When he arrived, he was informed by Branch Rickey (right) that the major league Dodgers were looking to sign a black player. Rickey explained to Robinson what he might have to face as the first black player in the majors in the twentieth century.

TO CANADA FIRST—Convinced that he had found the right man for his great experiment, Branch Rickey signed Robinson to a contract to play outside the U.S., for the Montreal Royals of the International League. In the Royals' first game of 1946, Robinson went four-for-five with one home run, stole two bases, and drove in four runs. Despite the racial hostilities that surfaced in some of the towns the Royals played in, Robinson continued to excel, finished the season with a .349 batting average and won the league's Most Valuable Player Award.

GOODBYE MONTREAL, HELLO BROOKLYN—The Brooklyn Dodgers' announce-ment in the spring of 1947 that Jackie Robinson would be playing in the majors that season resulted in an outcry of bigotry from some major league players. Numerous players signed petitions stating they would not play in any game with a Negro, and the St. Louis Cardinals even threatened to strike. Only the intervention of National League president Ford Frick and the threat of severe penalties for such actions prevented inci-dents from escalating.

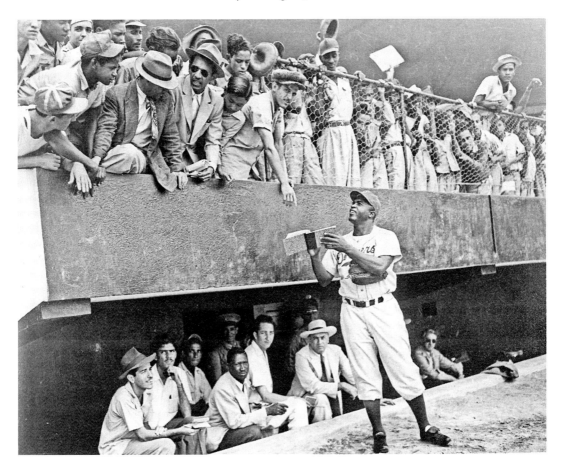

SIGN THIS!—To avoid possible racial hostilities in Florida, the Dodgers held spring training in Havana, Cuba. Rookie Robinson is shown signing autographs in 1947. The Dodgers had trained in Pensacola, Florida, the previous spring. In 1948, the Dodgers trained in the Dominican Republic. The following year, Branch Rickey built Dodgertown in Vero Beach, Florida. The camp was a self-contained facility where the black players and their families could live without interacting with the social ills of a sick society. Rickey's Dodgers had received bids to train in Santa Barbara or El Centro, California, but the cities offered no cash incentives.

VERO BEACH—The Robinsons, Jackie and Rachel, arrive by bus in Florida for the start of spring training in 1949.

Right: NEWK IN CUBA—Don Newcombe played two winters in Cuba: 1946-47 with Matanzas and 1948-49 with Marianao and Almendares.

Below: STEAL OF HOME—On June 24, 1947, Robinson became the first black player to steal home in a major league game. It was the first of 19 career steals of home. With his base running exploits, which were daring to say the least, Robinson stole 29 bases to lead the league that season. Robinson became renowned for his ability to unnerve pitchers by doing a jig, a jag and a hop ... up and down the baselines as they prepared to pitch.

JACKIE TAKES THE FIELD—In the first major league game to feature a black player, the Dodgers infielders appear in a jovial mood for the start of a tumultuous season. From left to right: Spider Jorgensen (3b), Pee Wee Reese (ss), Eddie Stanky (2b) and Jackie Robinson (1b). Robinson batted second in the lineup and played first base on his first day in the majors. Robinson made 11 putouts without an error. Future Hall of Fame umpire Al Barlick officiated at first base. The first major league pitcher he faced was the Boston Braves' 21-game winner, Johnny Sain. Robinson went hitless in three at-bats before 26,623 chilly fans.

FIRST ROY—Robinson won the first Rookie of the Year Award in 1947. Robinson proved to be very popular with fans. In fact, Negro Leagues teams that had been filling Yankee Stadium and Ebbets Field just a few years earlier were struggling to attract fans by 1948. The Negro Leagues' African American fan base eventually shifted to become diehard Dodgers fans when Robinson and other black players signed with Brooklyn.

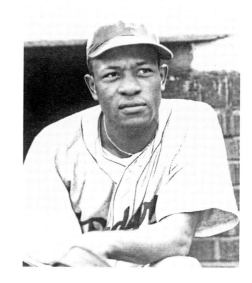

DANIEL ROBERT "DAN" BANKHEAD, 1947, 1950–1951, PITCHER—On August 26, 1947, he became the first black to pitch in the majors. In his debut, Bankhead joined an elite list of players who homered in their first big league at-bat, when he took Pittsburgh's Fritz Ostermueller yard. He would later pitch a seven-inning no-hitter (NH) against the Springfield Cubs for Class B for Nashua on July 25, 1948. That season Bankhead led the New England League in wins with 20.

STAFF MEETING—Jackie Robinson, Dan Bankhead and Don Newcombe receive words of wisdom from manager Burt Shotton, who had replaced the suspended Leo Durocher for the 1947 season. Bankhead played three seasons with the Dodgers, with his best year in 1950, at 30 years old, winning nine of 13 decisions. That season he started 12 games and had a 5.50 ERA. One of five Bankhead brothers to play in the Negro Leagues, Dan pitched in four East-West All-Star classics, picking up victories in the 1946 and 1947 contests.

ROOMIE—Before Dan Bankhead (left) joined Robinson (middle), on the Dodgers, Robinson was the sole African American on the team. Due to racial tensions at the time, Robinson was friendless on the Dodgers. When he hit his first major league home run on April 18, 1947, not a single Dodger shook his hand when Robinson returned to the dugout. Eventually, his talent, warm personality, and gutsy determination won over his teammates. Among the first friends was shortstop, and Kentucky native, Harold "Pee Wee" Reese. The man at right in the photograph is unidentified.

Top: KEYS TO THE KINGDOM—Jackie and Rachel Robinson receive car keys from tap dancer and former New York Black Yankees co-owner Bill "Bojangles" Robinson in Ebbets Field on September 23, 1947. The new ride was presented by Dodgers fans on "Jackie Robinson Day" as they celebrated their newly-clinched National League pennant. The Robinsons also received a television set, a $500 watch, an inter-racial goodwill plaque and cash gifts.

Bottom: CAMPY SIGNS—After Roy Campanella (left) was signed by Branch Rickey (right), he played for Nashua (1946) and later Montreal (1947) and St. Paul (1948). He won two minor league MVP Awards before the Dodgers called him to the big leagues.

IT'S OUT OF HERE—In 1948, Campanella began the season in the American Association with St. Paul, hitting 11 home runs in his first 24 games. By midseason, he was the Dodgers' regular catcher. Campy would hit 242 career home runs in ten seasons, with a high of 41 homers in 1953.

CAMPANELLA WITH MANAGER BURT SHOTTON—"More than one observer has likened Campanella's quickness behind the plate to that of a cat. He can pounce on bunts placed far out in front of the plate and he gets his throws away with no wasted motion. He has not only a rifle arm but an accurate one," wrote Tom Meany of the *New York World Telegram*.

READY FOR BATTLE—In 1951, Campanella won his first of three National League Most Valuable Player Awards while hitting .325 with 33 home runs and 108 RBI. His second MVP came in 1953, when he drove in a record (since broken) 142 runs as a catcher, and he grabbed a third MVP Award in 1955 after leading the Dodgers to their first World Series title.

JUNIOR GILLIAM, 1946–1950 WITH THE ELITE GIANTS—SECOND BASE-MAN—Gilliam started playing for the Baltimore Elite Giants at age 17. He played in four East-West All-Star Games and two major league All-Star Games. He is the only man to hit a home run in a Negro league (on 8-20-50, in Comiskey Park) and a major league (8-3-59, Los Angeles Memorial Coliseum) All-Star Game. Gilliam played two seasons in Montreal before coming to the Dodgers.

Top: THE ALL-STAR BARRIER IS BROKEN—On July 12, 1949, in Ebbets Field, the major leagues featured black players for the first time in the All-Star Game. From left to right, Roy Campanella, Larry Doby (American League), Don Newcombe and Jackie Robinson. The National Leaguers lost, 11–7, to their American League counterparts. *Bottom:* ALL STAR TICKET STUB.

FACE OFF—On July 8, 1949, Don Newcombe of the Dodgers (shown) and Hank Thompson of the Giants became the first black pitcher and batter to face each other in a game. That season, Newcombe led the National League with five shutouts and became the first black pitcher to win the Rookie of the Year Award. Newcombe's career included pitching in five World

BEST BUDS—Roy Campanella (left) and Don Newcombe celebrate in the clubhouse after Newcombe threw his third consecutive shutout in 1949. The 23-year-old Rookie of the Year won 17 games that season, with only eight losses. Newcombe became a 20-game winner three times, in 1951, 1955, and 1956.

DONALD "NEWK" NEWCOMBE, 1949–1951, MILITARY, 1954–1957, PITCHER—In 1951, Newcombe became the first African American pitcher to win 20 games in a season, and to lead either league in strikeouts with 164 whiffs. A workhorse of the staff, he pitched 32 innings over the last eight days of the 1951 season. He was not just an outstanding pitcher, but a fine hitter. In 1955, he hit a National League record seven home runs in 117 at-bats, while batting .359. To his left is renowned Memphis photographer Ernest Withers.

THIS YEAR'S MVP WINNER IS—Roy Campanella won his first MVP Award in 1951, capturing 243 vote points. In the process, he beat out Stan Musial (with 191), Monte Irvin (166), Sal Maglie (153), and teammates Preacher Roe (138) and Jackie Robinson (92). That season, Campy's numbers were .325/.393/.590, with 33 home runs and 108 RBIs.

Above and right: ROY CAM-
PANELLA LIQUORS—En
route to his 1951 National
League MVP Award, Cam-
panella opened a liquor store
on September 6, at 198 West
134th St., in Harlem. He purchased the store from Alfred
Moule for $9,000, for part
ownership. The opening night
gala included several celebri-
ties: Sugar Ray Robinson, Nat
King Cole, Joe Louis, Archie
Moore and Dodgers team-
mates.

SIGN ME UP—After an All-Star season and finishing 22nd in the 1951 MVP Award voting, along with a 20–9 won-lost record, Don Newcombe signs a contract for a reported $20,000 with Dodgers General Manager Emil Joseph "Buzzie" Bavasi, in December of 1951. Unfortunately, military duty called, and Big Newk was out of baseball for the entire 1952 and 1953 seasons.

JOSEPH BLACK—The 1952 Dodgers finished in first place of the National League with a 96–57 won-lost record. That year the Dodgers led the league in attendance with 1,088,704. Clockwise from top left are Joe Black, Pee Wee Reese, Jackie Robinson, manager Chuck Dressen, and Duke Snider. This was Black's rookie year, and he led the team in wins at 15 against four losses, with a 2.15 ERA. He was named Rookie of the Year and finished third in MVP Award voting behind Hank Sauer and Robin Roberts, but ahead of teammates Jackie Robinson, Pee Wee Reese, Duke Snider and Roy Campanella, who all finished in the top ten.

BIG JOE—Not pictured in Dodger blue is former Baltimore Elite Giant Joseph Black. In 1955, Dodger Black appeared in six games before being traded to the Cincinnati Redlegs. In Cincy, he posted a 5–2 won-lost record in 11 starts, with a 4.22 ERA. The 31-year-old Morgan State University grad would play for the Reds for two seasons.

JOE BLACK, 1952–1955, PITCHER— Black won the 1952 Rookie of the Year Award. On October 1, 1952, Black became the first black pitcher to win a World Series game. Few fans of the game know that Black became the first African American player with the Washington Senators in 1957, following the Cuban-born Carlos Paula in 1954.

GIVE ME SOME SKIN, MY FRIEND—Pee Wee Reese welcomes Junior Gilliam to the Dodgers in 1953. With 34-year-old Jackie Robinson spending time mostly in left field, second baseman Gilliam helped turn 102 double plays, while his partner at short, Reese, was involved in 83 double plays.

Right and Below: ROY CAMPANELLA, 1948–1957, CATCHER—Campanella was the first player to win three MVP Awards, in 1951, 1953, 1955. In 1951, Campy outpointed Stan "The Man" Musial, 243–191. In 1953, Campy won by a bigger margin with 297 points over runner-up Eddie Mathews' 216. His last MVP Award came at the expense of teammate Duke Snider. Snider's 221 points were edged out by Campy's 226.

When Brooklyn won its only world championship in 1955, Johnny Podres pitched a 2–0 shutout in the decisive seventh game and gave credit to his catcher. "That win was half Campy's," Podres said. "He never called a better game. He saw how my stuff was working and he seemed to know what the Yankee hitters were looking for."

THE REAL DEAL—Charlie Neal, from Longview, Texas, played for the Atlanta Black Crackers in the Negro Leagues for three months, while attending high school. He was signed by the Dodgers organization in 1949, before joining the team in 1956. In the 1959 World Series against the Chicago White Sox, he hit two home runs, drove in six runs and batted .370. After retirement from the field, he owned and operated the A.C. & T. Security Company in Dallas, Texas.

Opposite: 1955 WORLD CHAMPION DODGERS—From left to right: (front row) George Shuba, Don Zimmer, coach Joe Becker, coach Jake Pitler, manager Walt Alston, coach Billy Herman, Pee Wee Reese, Dixie Howell, Sandy Amoros and Roy Campanella; (middle row) clubhouse man J. Griffin, Carl Erskine, Sandy Koufax, traveling secretary Lee Scott (in suit), Roger Craig, Don Newcombe, Karl Spooner, Don Hoak, Carl Furillo, Frank Kellert, and trainer Harold "Doc" Wendler; (back row) Russ Meyer, Junior Gilliam, Billy Loes, Clem Labine, Gil Hodges, Ed Roebuck, Don Bessent, Duke Snider, Johnny Podres, Rube Walker and Jackie Robinson. The Bums won 98 of 153 games, an astounding 13½ games ahead of the Milwaukee Braves. The Dodgers were so dominating they led the National League in 11 offensive statistical categories. The Dodgers defeated the Yankees in seven games to claim the title. The winners received $9,768 each, while the losers got $5,599. The batboy, "Little Charlie" DiGiovanni (seated on ground), was the only Dodger with an open car to himself in the 1955 victory parade. Courtesy Dave Hochman.

SANDY AMOROS, 1952, 1954–1957, OUTFIELDER—In the seventh game of the 1955 World Series, Amoros snatched Yogi Berra's fly ball near the left-field stands in the sixth inning. Catching the Yankees off guard, he turned the catch into a double play, Amoros to Pee Wee Reese and Gil Hodges, that preserved Johnny Podres' 2–0 win over the Yankees. Because of that catch, the Bums of Brooklyn won their only championship in eight attempts.

CHRISTMAS IN OCTOBER—Dodgers teammates from left to right; Roy Campanella, Pee Wee Reese, Gil Hodges and Jackie Robinson. After losing the World Series to the New York Yankees in 1947, 1949, 1952, and 1953, Robinson and the Dodgers finally captured the World Championship in 1955. Although he only hit .182 in the series, Robinson scored five runs, including one tally as a result of stealing home in Game One.

NO-HITTERS GALORE—Campanella caught three no-hitters in his career, a record since broken. The first was on June 19, 1952, with Carl Erskine shutting out the Chicago Cubs, 5–0. The second no-no was on May 12, 1956. Again Erskine shut down the New York Giants, 3–0. Later that year on September 25, Sal Maglie and Campanella blanked the Philadelphia Phillies, 5–0.

JAMES WILLIAM "JUNIOR" GILLIAM, 1953–1957, SECOND BASEMAN—A true blue Dodger, Gilliam in his first year with the Bums led the league with 17 triples and drew 100 walks, while batting a respectable .278. For his efforts, he was named the 1953 National League Rookie of the Year, the fourth Dodger and sixth former Negro Leaguer to earn the honor.

Opposite, top: CONGRATULATIONS ... TRIPLETS—After posting a 27–7 won-lost season in 1956, Big Newk won the Cy Young and Most Valuable Player Awards, making him the first of only two pitchers to win all three major awards, Rookie of the Year, Cy Young and MVP, in his career. Detroit's Justin Verlander is the other. Newcombe finished his major league career at 34, with a 149–90 won-lost record and 3.56 ERA. Newcombe has one less win than Hall of Famer Dizzy Dean and a better lifetime ERA than two other Cooperstown honorees, Red Ruffing and Waite Hoyt. Without a doubt, Don Newcombe is a Hall of Famer.

Bottom: DON JUAN—Newcombe was popular with the ladies. Here, the former Newark Eagles pitcher entertains some smitten fans. In 1956, Newcombe won 27 games against only seven losses. In the process, he became the first player in major league history to be named winner of the both the Cy Young and MVP Awards in the same season.

1957 BOYS OF SUMMER—The last of the Brooklyn Bums. From left to right: (front row) Carl Erskine, Junior Gilliam, Clem Labine, Don Zimmer, Gino Cimoli, coach Billy Herman, coach Greg Mulleavy, Pee Wee Reese, manager Walt Alston, coach Joe Becker, coach Jake Pitler, Roy Campanella and Carl Furillo; (middle row) clubhouse attendant John Griffin, traveling secretary Lee Scott, Rene Valdez, Roger Craig, Randy Jackson, Bob Kennedy, Gil Hodges, Don Drysdale, Ed Roebuck, Don Bessent, Doc Wendler, unknown, and John Roseboro; (top row) Elmer Valo, Bill Harris, Danny McDevitt, Jackie Collum, Rube Walker, Joe Pignatano, Charlie Neal, Don Newcombe, Sandy Amoros, Johnny Podres, Duke Snider, Sandy Koufax, Fred Kipp and Jim Gentile. Seated on the ground are Charlie DiGiovanni, assistant to the clubhouse attendant (left), and batboy Eddie Lehan. The Dodgers finished with an 84–70 won-lost record, good enough for third place, 11 games behind the Milwaukee Braves. Courtesy Dave Hochman.

Opposite, top: ROY AND ROY, JR.—A happy father receives his first born, Roy Junior. Campy appeared in 32 World Series games, hitting four home runs, driving in 12 runs in 114 at bats, while batting .237. With respect to Ernie Banks, and later Buck O'Neil, the roly-poly, muscular Campanella was baseball's original goodwill ambassador.

Bottom: THREE KIDS AND THEIR DAD—Enjoying some quality time with Campy in 1957 are, left to right, Roy, II, Tony and two-year-old Ruth. Roy Campanella II became an award-winning director, writer, and producer, whose creative work includes mainstream television and independent feature films. His film, *The Company We Keep*, an ensemble romantic comedy set in the music industry, was honored with the Best Feature Film Award from the Urban MediaMakers Film Festival 2010. Roy II has directed several movies, including *Masquerade, Rendezvous,* and *Playing with Fire.*

JOHN ROSEBORO, 1957, CATCHER—In the year of the Chevy, Roseboro was only with the Brooklyn club one season before they moved to Los Angeles. Roseboro caught two of Sandy Koufax's no-hitters. According to writer Edward Gruver, "Koufax believed that he and Roseboro owned such a complete rapport 'it was as if there were only one mind involved.'"

TESTED—Bob Skinner of the Pittsburgh Pirates challenges John Roseboro. The catching talents of Roseboro are well known. Roseboro won a Gold Glove Award in 1961, making him the first black catcher in the National League to do so, and another in 1966. He played in three major league All-Star Games: 1961, 1962 and 1969. Roseboro also appeared in four World Series: 1959, 1963, 1965, and 1966.

Left: NEVER ON SUNDAY—At the age of 15, in 1937, Roy Campanella signed with the Baltimore Elite Giants of the Negro Leagues. Teammate Othello "Chico" Renfroe recalled that he was the "biggest fifteen-year-old boy I ever saw in my life." The team's shortstop, Thomas "Pee Wee" Butts, would get mad because Campanella would throw the ball so hard to second base during infield practice. As a youth, Campanella never thought of chasing a baseball career as his parents, devout Baptists, would not allow him to play on Sundays. Campanella once said, "You have to have a lot of little boy in you to play baseball for a living."

PERENNIAL ALL-STAR—Campanella made seven appearances in major league All-Star Games from 1949 to 1956. "Everyone talked about Roy's hitting, but his defense was just as impressive. He was cat-like for a guy of his size, and we were always in such agreement on pitch selection," claimed pitcher Clem Labine. On June 4, 1972, Campanella's uniform number, #39, was retired by the Dodgers organization.

THE ACCIDENT—Early on January 29, 1958, Campanella emerged from this car accident with a fractured fifth cervical vertebra, broken neck, and spinal cord damage. Returning home from his liquor store, he lost control of his car on the icy pavement. Tragically made a quadriplegic, Campy kept a positive attitude and an effervescent smile as a goodwill ambassador for the Dodgers organization for many years.

Campanella described the crash in a *Los Angeles Times* interview: "It had snowed a little that night, and the roads were a little wet and icy. I was about five minutes from my house when I hit some ice driving around a curve. I hit my brakes and the car slid across the road, hit a pole and turned over. I tried to reach up to turn the ignition off because I thought the car would catch fire, but I couldn't move my arm."

Opposite: CAMPANELLA'S SURGERY—Although he survived the crash, he suffered two fractured vertebrae. Five surgeons at Glen Cove Community Hospital worked four and a half hours to save his life. They succeeded in this, but his spine was permanently damaged; he remained paralyzed from the shoulders down. Shown at the rehab center in 1958 is Campanella being checked by Dr. Barnet Elkin (L) and attendant Leroy Newsome, at the Institute of Physical Medicine and Rehabilitation at the Bellevue Medical Center.

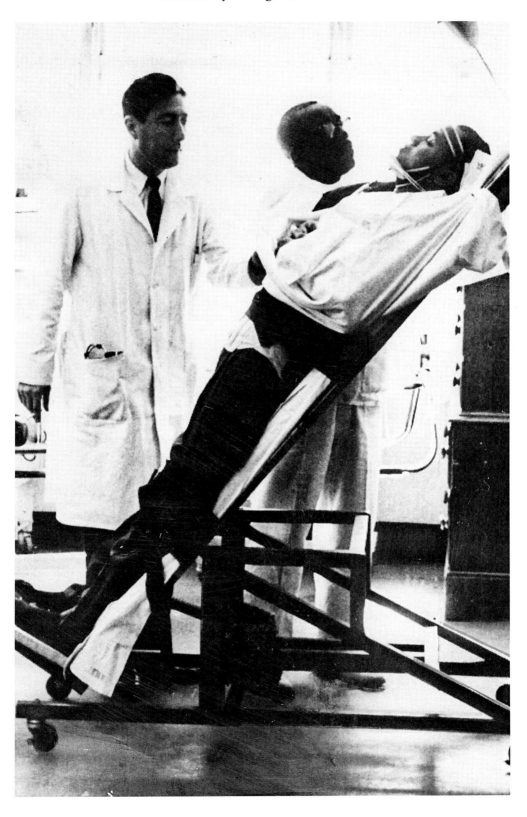

ROY CAMPANELLA WITH HIS KIDS—On October 1, 1958, months after his accident, Campanella with his kids, from left to right, Ruth, Tony and Roy II, appeared on Ralph Edwards' *This Is Your Life* show on NBC-TV.

FOUR YEARS LATER—Here in March of 1962, Campanella sits in his office at the Harlem liquor store. He could now move his shoulders, with some movement in his arms and hands. From his wheelchair, Campanella continued to do business, arranging speaking engagements with various civic and religious groups.

HIGH RISE—HIGH EXPECTATIONS—Roy Campanella is shown here at the Smith Houses in Manhattan on July 21, 1967, giving pointers to eight-year-old Larry McGarry (center) and 14-year-old Louis Lopez. New York Mets outfielder Tommy Davis assists. This was the first of 30 baseball clinics sponsored by the New York City Housing Authority. The Houses were named after four-time New York governor and 1928 Democratic presidential candidate Alfred E. Smith. Built in 1953, the 17-story high-rise complexes consisted of 12 buildings and contained 1,931 apartment units.

GOOD-BYE—On December 13, 1956, the Brooklyn Dodgers agreed to trade Robinson for New York Giants pitcher Dick Littlefield and $30,000. Robinson, seen here leaving the Dodgers' locker room for the last time, decided instead to retire from baseball. When Robinson retired, there were still three major league clubs that were not racially integrated: the Philadelphia Phillies, Detroit Tigers and Boston Red Sox.

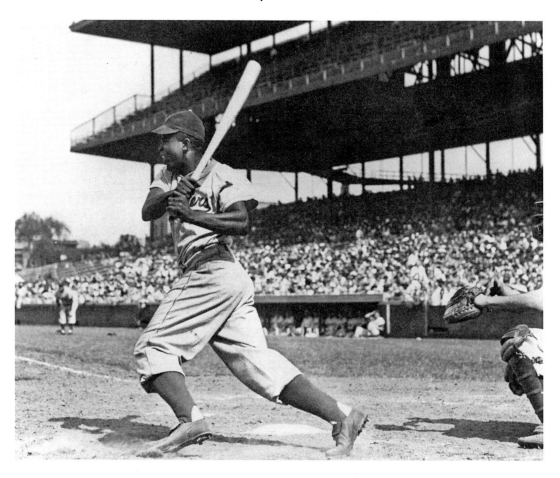

IT'S OVER!—The major league career of Jackie Robinson spanned ten years, 1382 regular season games, and six World Series. Robinson played in the outfield as well as at first base, second base, third base, and shortstop. He had a lifetime .311 average with the Dodgers while hitting 137 home runs and stealing 197 bases. He earned his highest salary in 1956, at $42,500. Upon retiring from the diamond, Robinson went to work at Chock Full O'Nuts, known for its coffee, as Vice President in charge of personnel relations.

JACKIE AND BUNNY—McKinley "Bunny" Downs started his Negro Leagues career in 1915 with the West Baden (IN) Sprudels, and later became business manager of the Indianapolis Clowns. As an official with the Clowns, he developed a young and shy Alabama lad named Hank Aaron. Upon retiring from baseball, Downs became supervisor of the Jackie Robinson Apartments in Flatbush.

GENDER BARRIER—Robinson may have broken major league baseball's color barrier, but Connie Morgan (on right), along with Toni Stone and Mamie "Peanuts" Johnson, broke the gender barrier in the Negro Leagues. Morgan, an outstanding basketball player from the Philadelphia area, played second base for the Indianapolis Clowns in 1954.

LAST CRY—"We wept, Brooklyn was a lovely place to hit. If you got a ball in the air, you had a chance to get it out. When they tore down Ebbets Field, they tore down a little piece of me," cried Duke Snider. Back on July 17, 1954, the Dodgers fielded the first black majority team in the majors, when they started five black players: Jim Gilliam at second base, Jackie Robinson at third, Sandy Amoros in left field, Don Newcombe on the mound and Roy Campanella catching.

Opposite, bottom: THE LAST STAND—Only 6,702 fans attended the final game at Ebbets Field on September 24, 1957. The Dodgers defeated the Pittsburgh Pirates, 2–0. Built by former Dodgers owner Charlie Ebbets in 1913, the field was razed on February 23, 1960. A seating capacity of less than 32,000 limited the big gates, driving owner Walter O'Malley to seek greener pastures. On October 8, the team officially announced the move to Los Angeles.

AUTHOR—After the release of the 1960 book, *Wait Till Next Year*, by acclaimed writer Carl Rowan, Jack Robinson celebrates with Elijah Muhammad (on right), founder of the Black Muslim party. To Robinson's left is Malcolm X. In March of 1963, Robinson wrote an open letter in the *NY Amsterdam News* criticizing the Rev. Adam Clayton Powell, Jr., in regards to Malcolm X: "In spite of the fact that you and I share deep respect for Minister Malcolm X as an individual … the way pointed by the Black Muslims is not the true way to the solution of the Negro problem."

Right: NUMBER 42—In 1962, Jack Roosevelt Robinson became the first African American to be inducted into the National Baseball Hall of Fame. He would go on to become an outspoken advocate for civil rights both on and off the diamond until his death on October 24, 1972, at the age of 53. In 1987, Major League Baseball renamed its Rookie of the Year Award the Jackie Robinson Award, and in 1997, all major league teams retired Robinson's number 42 in perpetuity.

PLAYERS WANT TO BE ENTERTAINERS—And entertainers want to be players. *Top:* Welterweight and middleweight champion Sugar Ray Robinson (left) gets some tips from Dodgers coach Cookie Lavagetto in 1950. Lavagetto would manage the Washington Senators from 1957 to 1960 and the Minnesota Twins in 1961. *Above:* Sugar Ray (right) with the Brown Bomber, Joe Louis, frequent visitors to Dodgers games.

SOLDIERS WITHOUT SWORDS—From left to right are *Afro-American* writer Sam Lacy, Dodgers pitcher Dan Bankhead, and *Chicago Defender* writer Wendell Smith. Both Lacy and Smith are winners of the Baseball Writers Association of America's J. G. Taylor Spink Award. They welded their mighty pens to change the mindset towards the integration of baseball with their editorials and stimulating articles. Courtesy Sam Lacy.

Opposite, top: JOE LOUIS—The boxer loved baseball too! On June 22, 1938, in Yankee Stadium, the Brown Bomber retained his heavyweight crown with a decisive knockout of Max Schmeling in the first round. Louis had won the title exactly one year earlier in Chicago when he knocked out James Braddock. This was his fourth defense of the title. Louis fought 27 fights in New York City, 17 times for the heavyweight title. His last fight in New York came on October 26, 1951, losing to Rocky Marciano in an eighth-round knockout.

    Bottom: ALI & JACKIE—Jackie Robinson jokingly hits a punching bag held by future heavyweight boxing champion Cassius Clay (later Muhammad Ali) at a New York gym during his visit on March 13, 1963.

♦ 11 ♦

New York Giants, 1949–1957

Hall of Famers	Halls of Fame and Induction Years
Monte Irvin	Mexico 1972, United States 1973
Willie Mays	United States 1979
Ray Noble	Cuba 1985
Artie Wilson	Puerto Rico 1993

Former Negro League Players, Team Years	Years, Major Negro League Teams
Monte Irvin, 1949–1955	1937–1948, Newark Eagles
Willie Mays, 1951–1952, 1954–1957	1948–1950, Birmingham Black Barons
Ray Noble, 1951–1953	1945–1948, New York Cubans
	1949, New Jersey Giants
	1950, Oakland Oaks
Hank Thompson, 1949–1956	1943–1948, Kansas City Monarchs
Artie Wilson, 1951	1944–1948, Birmingham Black Barons

Most Valuable Player

Willie Mays, 1954, 1965

Rookie of the Year

Willie Mays, 1951

Retired Numbers of Former Negro League Players

Willie Mays, #24 (by the San Francisco Giants)
Monte Irvin #20 (by the San Francisco Giants)
Jackie Robinson #42 (by Major League Baseball)

Opposite, top: POLO GROUNDS—The park famously known for this unusual shape once stood on Manhattan's East 159th Street, between Coogan's Bluff and the Harlem River. Built in 1911 by New York Giants owner John T. Brush, it was the city's first concrete-and-steel park, seating roughly 16,000 fans, initially. Former Negro Leaguers like Homestead Grays first baseman Luke Easter (in 1948) and Hank Aaron (in 1962), along with Joe Adcock and Lou Brock, are the only players to hit a ball into the center field bleachers, an estimated blast of more than 500 feet.

THE LIP TALKS—Willie Mays said in a personal interview, "Leo Durocher was like my father away from home. I first met Leo in Sanford, Florida. When I went to California I stayed with Leo in his house. His kid, Chris Durocher, was my roommate on the road. Chris would go to the black areas and stay with me. Leo trusted me. He knew that if his kid was going to stay with me, nothing was going to happen to that kid. When we used to eat soul food, he didn't know what it was. We had black-eyed peas, cornbread, chitlins, and he was used to eating steaks! He goes back and he tells his father, 'I had cornbread,' and his father started laughing."

MONTE IRVIN SAYS—In a personal interview, he stated, "It was in 1942 and I flew from St. Louis to Mexico City. I had just gotten married and we were on our honeymoon. I hit .397 and led the Mexican League with 20 home runs and was named the MVP of the league. It's then I realized I could compete with anyone at any level."

MONTE IRVIN, 1949–1955, OUTFIELDER—In 1951, Irvin became the first African American player to lead the National League in RBI with 121. That season, he hit .312 (fifth in the league), with 11 triples (third) and 24 home runs (tenth).

PUTTING ON GIANTS CAPS IN 1949—"I was thrilled. It was the greatest moment in my career at the time. I was fortunate to be given a chance, as I was almost 30 years old. Hank and I reported the first week in July of 1949. We met Leo Durocher and he called a team meeting. He said, 'Fellas, I want you to meet Monte Irvin and Hank Thompson. These men have fine records in the International League and this is all I am going to say: If they can play baseball and help this club, help us put some money in our pockets, then we want them with the Giants. We think they can help us, they're members of this team and that's all I'm going to say about race. Go out, let these guys play and treat them just like you would anybody else.' Consequently, we had no problem with any of our teammates. What problems we did have were from some of the fans in some places we played," recalled Monte Irvin.

WILLIE HOWARD "SAY HEY" MAYS, 1951–1952, MILITARY, 1954–1957, OUT-
FIELDER—Before coming to the Giants, he appeared in 35 games for the 1951 Minneapolis Millers, hitting .477 and slugging .799. Note that his locker is next to future
Hall of Fame third baseman Ray Dandridge. Despite leading the Millers to the championship and being named the league's Most Valuable Player in 1950, Dandridge never
got his cup of coffee in the majors. Courtesy Minnesota Historical Society.

DYNAMIC DUO—Mentor Monte Irvin (age 32), at left, and mentee Willie Mays (20) were teammates in 1951. Respectively, they hit .312 and .274, with 24 and 20 home runs, plus 121 and 68 RBIs. Irvin's 121 RBIs were the first time an African American led either league. They helped lead the Giants to a first-place finish, winning 98 games against 59 losses.

UNCLE SAM CALLS—Here a 21-year-old Willie Mays, at the First Army Recruiting Headquarters in New York, waves at friends. Mays is scheduled to report to Camp Kilmer in New Jersey the last week of May 1952.

MVP—Mays won the 1954 National League's Most Valuable Player Award. That season, the former Black Baron led the league with a .345 average, a .667 slugging percentage, and 13 triples. He hit 41 homers that season, third in the league. Mays would repeat as the NL's MVP in 1965.

ARTHUR "ARTIE" LEE WILSON, 1951, SHORTSTOP—THE LAST .400 HITTER—In 1948, Artie Wilson, playing for the Birmingham Black Barons, hit .402 to lead the Negro American League in batting. He produced 134 hits in 333 at-bats, scored 41 runs and drove in 41 teammates. The next season, 1949, he won the Pacific Coast League batting crown with a nifty .348 average, plus the stolen base title with 46. Between seasons, the slap hitter led the Puerto Rican Winter League in hits with 126 while playing for Mayaguez.

CUP OF COFFEE—The 30-year-old Artie Wilson had only 22 major league at-bats with the 1951 Giants. He played three games at shortstop, three games at second base and two games at first base. The left-handed slap hitter, who hit to the opposite field, appeared in seven East-West All-Star Games at shortstop during his Negro Leagues days.

RAFAEL MIGUEL "RAY" NOBLE, 1951–1953, CATCHER—A 32-year-old rookie, Ray Noble was the backup catcher for Wes Westrum during the Giants' "miracle" 1951 pennant drive. Noble appeared in two World Series games, and was hitless in two at bats. In three seasons with the Giants, he appeared in 107 games, getting 243 at-bats. Noble batted .218 with nine homers and 40 RBIs during his major league career. Noble spent four seasons, 1945–1948, with the N.Y. Cubans and was inducted into the Cuban Hall of Fame in 1985. Courtesy Wayne Stivers.

HENRY CURTIS "HANK" THOMPSON, 1949–1956, OUTFIELDER—From 1943 to 1948, Thompson played for the Kansas City Monarchs. After the 1948 season, Thompson was off to Cuba for winter baseball, when he received word that the N.Y. Giants wanted to send him and Monte Irvin to Jersey City in the International League. Thompson signed for $2,500. At Jersey City, he hit .303 with 12 home runs and stole 11 bases in 55 games. Overall, it was a solid all-around year for Thompson. As for his greatest moment in the Majors? Thompson said, "*In 1950, I participated in 43 double plays. No National League third baseman, white or black, has ever been in so many.*"

SAY HEY, HERE I AM—During his days with the Birmingham Black Barons (1948–1950) Mays wanted to be a shortstop, but with prospective league batting champion Artie Wilson hitting around .400, Mays was shoved to the outfield. That season, the 17-year-old high school senior appeared in only 25 games and batted .262. His line stats included 22 hits in 84 at-bats, with three doubles, a homer and seven RBIs.

Opposite, top: THE FOUR HORSEMEN OF 1951—The nucleus of a championship team included, from left to right, catcher Ray Noble, shortstop Artie Wilson, left fielder Monte Irvin and third baseman Hank Thompson.

Bottom: A TRIVIA FIRST FOR OUTFIELDERS—On October 3, 1951, with the New York Giants trailing the Brooklyn Dodgers, 4–1, in the ninth inning, Don Mueller singled Alvin Dark to third base. With one out, Whitey Lockman doubled to score Dark, but Mueller tore ankle tendons sliding into third and was carried from the field. Their teammate, Bobby Thomson, would hit the "shot heard around the world" propelling the Giants into the World Series. The next day, in Yankee Stadium, Hank Thompson took his injured teammate's spot in right field, alongside Willie Mays (center) and Monte Irvin (left), thereby creating the first African American outfield. The Giants would go on to lose the World Series to the Yankees, four games to two.

NEW YORK GIANTS
1954

WILLMONT LIQUORS—After the 1954 Series ended, Willie Mays and Monte Irvin opened Willmont Liquors, located on Pennsylvania Avenue in Brooklyn. Irvin explained, "Mays and I put up our World Series winnings of $11,000 each for this store in a Jewish neighborhood. We wanted to move to Harlem until the SLA [State Liquor Authority] blocked the transfer of all liquor stores." Irvin added, "We hired Howard Cosell as our lawyer. Unable to move, we sold the store the following year for a loss." Courtesy Monte Irvin.

Opposite, top: SPRING TRAINING 1954—The Giants and the Cleveland Indians met in sunny Arizona for spring training. Seated, left to right: Hank Thompson (Giants), Dave Hoskins, Larry Doby and Al Smith (Indians); Willie Mays and Ruben Gomez (Giants), and Jose Santiago (Indians). Standing are writer Sam Lacy and Monte Irvin (Giants). All these athletes were products of the Negro Leagues except pitcher Ruben Gomez. Courtesy Sam Lacy.

Bottom: 1954 GIANTS—Going into the World Series as 2–1 underdogs, the 1954 Giants became the first integrated major league team to win a World Championship. The black players are: Hank Thompson (front row, second from right), Willie Mays (middle row, fourth from left), Monte Irvin (middle row, seventh from left), and Ruben Gomez (middle row, second from right). They won 97 games and lost 57 to win the National League title by five games over the Dodgers. They swept the Cleveland Indians and their powerful pitching staff in the World Series. The presumably unbeatable Indians had won a record 111 games that season.

THERE GOES MY CAP, AGAIN—Mays was the first player to hit 300 homers and steal 300 bases (338 total). He led the National League in steals four consecutive seasons with his daring base running style. An outstanding center fielder, Mays is the only outfielder with more than 7,000 career putouts (7,095). When the Gold Glove Award was created in 1957, Mays earned one each of the first 12 years.

THE MAYS FAMILY—Willie Mays and his wife Marghuerite proudly show off their five-week-old adopted son, Michael. They are shown here in spring training in Phoenix in 1959.

SEPARATION PAPERS—In 1961, waiting for her lawyer, Mrs. Marghuerite Wendell Chapman Mays filed for separation and eventual divorce. They had started dating in 1955 and married a year later.

DO YOU REMEMBER WHEN?— Irvin recalls with Roy Campanella the 1951 playoff game, in which Bobby Thomson hit the "shot heard around the world." In that historic game, Rube Walker was the Dodgers' catcher, not Campanella. Irvin thought Campy had a sprained ankle, but later found out from his buddy that the Dodgers were resting him for the first game of the Series against the Yankees. Perhaps Ralph Branca would have thrown a different pitch to Thomson if Campanella had been behind the plate.

RETURNING HOME—Visiting Shea Stadium in June of 1969, now a star in San Francisco, Willie Mays shared some laughs with Pearl Bailey, who was performing in the musical *Hello Dolly* on Broadway, along with Mrs. Gil Hodges (center).

Opposite, top: NUMBER 42 AND NUMBER 24—A rare image of mirrored greatness together, Jackie Robinson and Willie Mays. Perhaps they were sharing some strategies to help the National League defeat the American League in the midsummer All-Star Game. Mays said, "Robinson was important to all blacks. To make it into the majors and to take all the name calling, he had to be something special. He had to take all this for years, not just for Jackie Robinson, but for the nation."

Bottom: BIG HANDS—On April 30, 1961, as a San Francisco Giant, Mays hit four home runs against the Milwaukee Braves. The new celebrity was later flown to New York to appear on the "Ed Sullivan Show." In 2015, at age 84, Mays was awarded the Presidential Medal of Freedom by President Barack Obama.

Above: MAE LOUISE ALLEN—Ms. Allen married Mays in 1971 and died in 2013. This 1974 image shows the couple at their home in Atherton, California. Mays, 43 years old, had recently signed an eight-year contract with the New York Mets to help train newcomers to the team.

Left: BLACK ATHLETES HALL OF FAME—In March of 1974, Mrs. Rachel Robinson, widow of Jackie Robinson, joined Willie Mays for induction ceremonies at the first annual Black Athletes Hall of Fame dinner in New York City. Rachel's late husband and Mays were among 30 athletes inducted that evening.

ROBINSON AND MAYS REUNITE—Jackie Robinson congratulates Willie Mays on his Giants winning the 1954 World Series. In his book, *I Never Had It Made*, Robinson wrote, "I don't think anyone in or out of sports could ever seriously accuse Willie Mays of offending white sensitivities. But when he was in California, whites refused to sell him a house in their community. They loved his talent but they didn't want him for a neighbor."

MONTE IRVIN WAVING—After the 1956 season, the cerebral Irvin traded his bat for a pen, scouted for the New York Mets from 1967 to 1968 and later spent 17 years (1968–1984) as a public relations specialist to the commissioner's office, mostly under Bowie Kuhn's administration. Irvin served on the Veterans' Committee of the Hall of Fame and actively campaigned for recognition of deserving Negro Leagues veterans, until they disbanded after the 2001 elections.

WILLIE MAYS IN HIS GLORY—Mays joined the Minneapolis Millers of the American Association in 1951. After 35 games in AAA, the Say Hey Kid was burning up the league with a .477 average, eight home runs and 18 doubles, in 149 at-bats. Mays' all-star performance enticed the Giants to call him up to the Show. The colorful Willie Mays finished the 1951 season with the parent club. He hit for a .274 average, with 20 homers and 68 RBIs in 121 games, and was named the National League Rookie of the Year, getting 18 of 24 votes cast.

MONTE IRVIN SWINGING FOR THE FENCES—*"Monte was our best young ball-player at the time.... He could do everything. You see, we wanted men who could go there and hit the ball over the fence, and Monte could do that. He could hit that long ball, he had a great arm, he could field, he could run. Yes, he could do everything. It's not that Jackie Robinson wasn't a good ballplayer; but we wanted Monte because we knew what he could do. But after Monte Irvin went to the Army and came back, he was sick* [inner ear problem], *and then they passed him up and looked for somebody else,"* lamented James "Cool Papa" Bell.

♦ 12 ♦

New York Yankees,
1955–1959

"There is no room in baseball for discrimination. It is our national pastime and a game for all."—Yankees slugger Lou Gehrig

With the last major league team, the Boston Red Sox, integrating their roster with Pumpsie Green and Earl Wilson, in 1959, the story of black baseball ends here. From 1955 to 1959, the Yankees featured three men of color: Elston Howard, who debuted in 1955, Harry Simpson in 1957, and two years later, Hector Lopez from Panama.

Former Negro League Players, Team Years	*Years, Negro League Teams*
Elston Howard, 1955–1967	1948–1953, Kansas City Monarchs
Harry Simpson, 1957–1958	1946–1948, Philadelphia Stars

Most Valuable Player

Elston Howard, 1963

Rookies of the Year

No former Negro Leaguers

Retired Number of Negro Leagues Player

Elston Howard, #32
Jackie Robinson #42 (by Major League Baseball)

Left: WILLIAM "DIZZY" DISMUKES—Dismukes has been credited as being the first black scout for the Yankees. A former submarine pitcher in the Negro Leagues, he is credited with hurling two no-hitters. The dapper Dismukes managed the Detroit Wolves in the 1932 East-West League and later became business manager for the Kansas City Monarchs.

Below: BROTHERHOOD—The first Negro Leagues game played in Yankee Stadium occurred on July 5, 1930. The doubleheader pitted the New York Lincoln Giants against the Baltimore Black Sox, with the proceeds going to the Brotherhood of Sleeping Car Porters. The manager of the Lincoln Giants, 46-year-old John Henry "Pop" Lloyd, went 4-for-8 that day with a sacrifice, a stolen base, and 24 putouts at first base with one error.

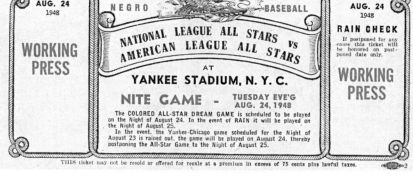

COLORED ALL-STAR DREAM GAME—Not to be confused with the East-West All-Star game played annually in Chicago was the all-star game between the National and American League teams. Shown are tickets for the grandstand, bleachers and press corps from the third annual event. The Nationals won, 6–1, with Newark Eagles pitcher Max Manning picking up the win. Luis Marquez, center fielder for the Homestead Grays, hit a 330-foot homer over the right field fence with Frank Austin on first. To represent New Yorkers, Minnie Minoso of the Cubans hit two doubles, George Crowe of the Black Yankees had a single, and Cubans ace Dave Barnhill pitched three scoreless innings. Of the 31 participants, a dozen men would later play in the major leagues.

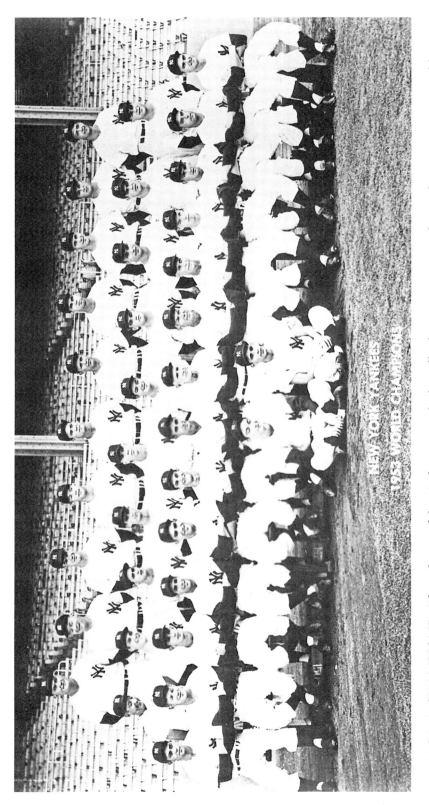

NEW YORK YANKEES
1953 WORLD CHAMPIONS

1953 WORLD CHAMPIONS—This edition of the Yankees were the last all-white team in major league history to win a World Series. From left to right: (front row) Art Schallock, Whitey Ford, Billy Martin, Phil Rizzuto, Yogi Berra, Steve Kraly, coach Frank Crosetti, manager Casey Stengel, coach Bill Dickey, coach Jim Turner, Gil McDougald, Irv Noren, Gene Woodling and Charles Silvera; (middle row) trainer Gus Mauch, Jim McDonald, Willy Miranda, Jerry Coleman, Bob Kuzava, Bill Miller, Tom Gorman, Bill Renna, Gus Triandos and Vic Raschi; (back row) Johnny Mize, Ed Lopat, Andy Carey, Mickey Mantle, Hank Bauer, Ralph Houk, Johnny Sain, Don Bollweg, Allie Reynolds, and Joe Collins. The bat boys are Joe Carrieri (left) and Iggy Manzidelis. The Yanks won 99 of 151 games and defeated the Dodgers, four games to two, in the World Series. Courtesy Wayne Stivers.

Left: CASEY STENGEL—Stengel was the first Yankees manager to have a black player, Elston Howard. The outspoken Stengel chimed in to sportswriter Robert W. Creamer about the signing of Howard, "When I finally get a nigger, I get the only one who can't run." The former Brooklyn Dodger hit the first home run (an in-side-the-parker) at the opening of Ebbets Field in 1913. An out-standing strategist, Stengel won a record 37 World Series games as manager, to match his uni-form number. Despite his initial thoughts about black players, Stengel was a great manager who overcame his bias afflic-tions.

Above, right: SAN JUAN'S ELSTON HOWARD—The New York Yankees signed rookie Howard for the 1955 season, but here he pondered the ques-tion of which glove he would wear, a catcher's mitt or a fielder's glove, for the San Juan Senadores in the Puerto Rican Winter League.

ELSTON GENE "ELLIE" HOWARD, 1955–1967, CATCHER—On November 7, 1963, Howard was named the American League's Most Valuable Player, becoming the league's first black player to win the award. *"I just won the Nobel Prize of baseball,"* shouted a normally cool Howard. In 1984, Howard's uniform number #32 was retired by the Yankees.

Opposite, bottom: ELSTON HOWARD, 1948–1953, CATCHER WITH THE MONARCHS—Later, Howard would win Gold Glove Awards for his catching in 1963 and 1964. Howard played in nine consecutive all-star games, from 1957 to 1965. In 1958, for his World Series–winning single in the 8th inning of Game Seven, Howard became the first catcher to win the Babe Ruth Award, established in 1949 in memory of Babe Ruth's death, presented by the New York chapter of the Baseball Writers' Association of America (BBWAA).

HARRY LEON "SUITCASE" SIMPSON, 1957–1958, OUTFIELDER, FIRST BASEMAN—Voted to the 1956 All-Star Game as a Kansas City Athletic, Simpson finished 11th in the MVP voting, enticing a trade to the Yankees in June of 1957. In June of 1958, the Yankees traded him back to the A's with Bob Grim, for Duke Maas and Virgil Trucks. The former Negro Leagues star for the Philadelphia Stars was nicknamed "Suitcase" as he played for several teams during his eight major league seasons.

Opposite, bottom: OH SAY, CAN YOU SEE?—Yankee Stadium may be known as the "House that Ruth Built," but Babe Ruth does not hold the record for the longest home run hit in the park. According to *The Sporting News* of June 3, 1967, that record belongs to Negro Leagues slugger and Hall of Fame catcher Josh Gibson. Gibson's record blast, the paper reported, struck the center field wall behind the bleachers, a distance of 580 feet from home plate. Ruth may have built it, but Gibson was the landlord.

HECTOR HEADLEY LOPEZ, 1959–1966, OUTFIELDER, THIRD BASEMAN—A native of Colon, Panama, he had his best season in 1959, finished in the top ten in slugging percentage, hits, doubles and RBI. During his Yankees years, he was often the third outfielder in the Roger Maris and Mickey Mantle rotation that won two of the five consecutive World Series they played in from 1960 to 1964. In 1969, Lopez made history and became the first black manager at the Triple-A level while managing the Buffalo Bisons, six years before Frank Robinson became the first black manager in Major League Baseball.

JOSHUA GIBSON—According to a letter written to Philip Ross in 1999 by Philadelphia Stars second baseman Mahlon Duckett, "Yes it's true, as I was there! Josh hit a home run out of Yankee Stadium over the third deck off of our pitcher Henry McHenry. The drive, they said wasn't measured but it had to be over 600 feet."

COLORED WORLD SERIES CLASSIC—Not really! There was only one league in 1934, the Negro National League, with the Chicago American Giants finishing in first place, followed by the Philadelphia Stars. On this date, there was a four-team doubleheader. The Pittsburgh Crawfords, who finished third in the league, defeated the Philadelphia Stars, 3–1. In the second game, the New York Black Yankees beat the league champion American Giants, 3–2, in six innings.

RAIN CHECK FOR GAME K—Signed by Negro National League president Thomas T. Wilson. In 1933, big-time black baseball turned the financial corner with Gus Greenlee and Tom Wilson at the helm. They organized a new Negro National League on a firmer financial footing than had ever been known in Negro baseball. In the spring of 1933, Wilson proposed to Greenlee and Robert Cole of Chicago that they jointly sponsor a showcase for the league's all-star talent. Thus, the East-West All Star Classic was born—a game which from the start proved to be among the most successful continuing sports promotions in American history.

Opposite: THE GLOBETROTTERS IN HAWAII—The West Coast Negro Baseball League was created on October 18–20, 1945, at the Elks Club in Oakland, with Abe Saperstein named owner of the Seattle Steelheads. The Steelheads were a spin-off of Saperstein's Globetrotters baseball team, which debuted in 1944. Shown here are the trotters during a 1946 tour of Honolulu. From left to right; Unknown, Herb Simpson, Luke Easter (from Saperstein's Cincinnati Crescents), Sherwood Brewer, Piper Davis, Walter Burch, Ulysses Redd, Abe Saperstein, Johnny Markham and speedster Jesse Owens. According to Brewer, Owens would spot him and Simpson ten yards and beat them in the 100-yard dash. These globetrotters barnstormed throughout the Northwest, never setting foot in New York City. Courtesy Sherwood Brewer.

♦ 13 ♦

Harlem Globetrotters

HARLEM GLOBETROTTERS BASEBALL TEAM—The Original Harlem Globetrotters of 1927, the basketball kings, never played a game in Harlem until 1968, more than 40 years after their incarnation. These baseball globetrotters who shared the Harlem name were just as guilty of commercialism of the black identifier, as they never visited Sugar Hill.

JAMES FISHBAUGH—He was a second baseman for the Globetrotters in 1948 and 1949. Fishbaugh later played for the Asheville (NC) Blues and the Chicago American Giants.

SHERWOOD BREWER—He spent most of his career with the Indianapolis Clowns and the Kansas City Monarchs, and served as the Monarchs' manager in 1960. A shortstop and second baseman, Brewer played in four East-West All-Star Games.

1949 HARLEM GLOBETROTTERS PITCHING STAFF—The aces from left to right: Boots Moore, Frank "Big Pitch" Carswell, Joe Bankhead, Laymon Ramsey, Johnny Williams and Henry Rateree. In 1945, as a Cleveland Buckeye, Carswell pitched a four-hit shutout against the Homestead Grays to complete a four-game sweep for the World Championship.

1949 HARLEM GLOBETROTTERS OUTFIELDERS—Leaping from left to right: Sonny Smith (utility), Zell Miles (rf), and brothers Leon (cf) and Sam "Boom Boom" Wheeler (lf). Smith also played for the Chicago American Giants and the original hardwood Globetrotters. Sam Wheeler also played basketball with the Globetrotters and the Harlem Magicians. Wheeler made a brief appearance with the New York Cubans in 1948.

HERBERT "BRIEFCASE" SIMPSON, 1948, FIRST BASEMAN—Perhaps the most talented player on the Harlem club was Herb Simpson, shown here with manager Paul Hardy, catching, and pitcher Rogers Pierre looking on. From 1942 to 1951, Simpson also played for the Birmingham Black Barons, Chicago American Giants, and Homestead Grays.

DID DUTY MISS TAG ON GIBSON?—No! Josh Gibson is tagged out at home by Ted "Double Duty" Radcliffe in the fourth inning of the 1944 East-West All-Star Game at Chicago's Comiskey Park. The colorful Radcliffe acquired his nickname because he could pitch one game of a double-header and catch the other game. Double Duty played and managed the Globetrotters in the mid–1940s. Radcliffe also played for the Brooklyn Eagles (1935) and the New York Black Yankees (1933).

PAUL JAMES HARDY, 1947, CATCHER—Hardy closed out his professional career with the Globetrotters. He was an outstanding receiver with several teams, including the Satchel Paige All-Stars in 1939, the Kansas City Monarchs, Chicago American Giants, Birmingham Black Barons and Memphis Red Sox.

NAPOLEON "NAP" GULLEY, 1945, 1948, PITCHER, OUTFIELDER—He was a left-handed pitcher with an outstanding curveball. Gulley played with several teams, including the Chicago American Giants, Birmingham Black Barons, Cleveland Buckeyes and the Newark Eagles. In 1950, he was signed by the Brooklyn Dodgers organization, but switched to the Chicago Cubs' Class C team, the Visalia Cubs of the California League, as an outfielder for four of the next five seasons, producing some quality offensive seasons.

ULYSSES ADOLPH "HICKEY" REDD, 1947, SHORTSTOP—Redd could play all the infield positions, but shortstop was his best spot. The Baton Rouge native was the infield anchor for Birmingham Black Barons in the early 1940s. Redd also played for the Chicago American Giants and the Cincinnati Crescents.

♦ 14 ♦

New York Black Travelers

NEW YORK BLACK TRAVELERS—Owned and operated by the former New York Black Yankees officer and secretary to the Negro National League, Curtis A. Leaks, the team played one season, 1950, with all of its games outside of New York City.

NEW YORK BLACK TRAVELERS BATTERY—Pictured is the battery of Julius Bowers (left) and Roy Lee Chapman (right). Chapman also pitched for the New York Black Yankees in 1949 and 1950.

♦ 15 ♦

Harlem Stars

1949 NEW YORK HARLEM STARS—Visiting Caracas, Venezuela, is the all-star team of non–New Yorkers. From left to right are: (front row) James "Bus" Clarkson, Lloyd "Duckie" Davenport, Ray Neil, Felix McLaurin, Othello "Chico" Renfroe, and Howard Easterling; (back row) Unknown man in suit, Stanley Glenn, Andy "Pullman" Porter, Gready "Lefty" McKinnis, Walter "Buck" Leonard, Pat Scantlebury, Bob Griffin, Art "Superman" Pennington, and Emory Long. Courtesy Art Pennington.

1955 DICK LUNDY'S NEW YORK BLACK YANKEES—This team was based out of Jacksonville, Florida, where Lundy lived. The former all-star shortstop (two appearances in the East-West classic) managed the 1929 Baltimore Black Sox to an American Negro League championship. This team photograph was taken on May 29 at Griffith Stadium, as they prepared to play the Indianapolis Clowns. Appearing, left to right: (top row) Aubrey Grigsby, Jim Proctor (later a Detroit Tigers pitcher in 1959), Chink McCoy, Leon Diggs, Shedrick Green, [Rev.] Cliff Layton, unknown, Billy "Beaver" Harris; bottom row, ? Miranda, Orlando "Leo" Lugo, Eldridge Harris, unknown, Donald Fearbry, Joe Elliott, Albert Jeffcoat. IDs courtesy Lionel Evelyn.

East-West All-Stars Representing New York–Based Teams

Note: (2) designates that a player appeared in both games that year. In some years, only one East-West All-Star game was scheduled. See the author's *Black Baseball National Showcase: The East-West All-Star Game, 1933–1953* for game details for each player.

BROOKLYN EAGLES—
Four players

1935

Day, Leon.
Giles, Sr., George Franklin 1b
Jenkins, Clarence R. "Fats" lf
Stone, Edward "Ed, Ace" ph

NEW YORK BLACK YANKEES—
18 players

1933

Jenkins, Clarence R. "Fats" lf

1937

Brown, Barney "Brinquitos"

1938

Brown, Barney "Brinquitos"
Cannady, Walter I. "Rev" 3b

1939

Holland, Elvis William "Bill"
McDuffie, Terris "The Great"

1940

Barker, Marvin "Hank, Hack" cf, rf
Clarke, Robert "Eggie"
Seay, Richard William "Dickie" 2b

1941

Kimbro, Henry Allen "Jimbo" cf
Seay, Richard William "Dickie" 2b

1942

Smith, Eugene L. "Gene"
Wilson, Daniel Richard "Dan" lf (2)

1945

Barker, Marvin "Hank, Hack" 3b

1947

Hayes, John William "Johnny" c (2)

1948

Barker, Marvin "Hank, Hack" ph
Crowe, George Daniel "Big George" 1b
Griffith, Robert Lee "Schoolboy"

NEW YORK CUBANS—
43 players

1935

Dihigo, Martin p cf
Oms, Alejandro "Walla Walla" rf
Tiant, Sr., Luis Eleuterio "Sir Skinny"

1939

Lopez, Candido Justo "Cando, Police Car" lf

1940

Crespo, Alejandro "Home Run" lf
Martinez, Horacio "Rabbit" ss
Ruiz, Silvino "Poppa"

1941

Barnhill, Dave "Impo"

233

Coimbre, Francisco Atiles "Pancho" rf
Martinez, Horacio "Rabbit" ss

1942

Barnhill, Dave "Impo" p (2)
Blanco, Herberto "Harry" 2b, p (2)
Vargas, Juan Estando "Tetelo" cf (2)

1943

Barnhill, Dave "Impo"
Martinez, Horacio "Rabbit" 2b
Vargas, Juan Estando "Tetelo" cf

1944

Coimbre, Francisco Atiles "Pancho" rf
Howard, Carranza "Schoolboy"
Martinez, Horacio "Rabbit" ss
Morris, Barney "Big Ad"

1945

Dihigo, Martin.
Linares, Rogelio "Ice Cream" rf
Martinez, Horacio "Rabbit" ss

1946

Diaz, Pedro "Manny" ph
Garcia, Silvio ss
Louden, Louis Oliver "Tommy"

Scantlebury, Patricio Athlestan "Pat" p, ph
(2)

1947

Duany, Claro rf, ph (2)
Garcia, Silvio 2b (2)
Louden, Louis Oliver "Tommy" c (2)
Minoso, Saturnino Orestes Arrieta "Minnie" 3b (2)
Tiant, Sr., Luis Eleuterio "Sir Skinny" p (2)

1948

Barnhill, Dave "Impo"
Louden, Louis Oliver "Tommy" c (2)
Minoso, Saturnino Orestes Arrieta "Minnie" 3b (2)

1949

Diaz, Pedro "Manny" cf
Easterling, Howard 3b
Scantlebury, Patricio Athlestan "Pat"

1950

Diaz, Pedro "Manny"
Galata, Raul
Gonzalez, Hiram "Rene" 1b
Louden, Louis Oliver "Tommy"
Scantlebury, Patricio Athlestan "Pat"

New York State Cemeteries

(burial sites of former Negro Leagues players)

Beverly Hills Cemetery, Lake Mohegan, NY
Fiall, George Goodwin; 1900–1936

Calvary Cemetery, Queens, NY
Torriente, Cristobal (Carlos); 1893–1938

Calverton National Cemetery, Calverton, NY
Brown, James Philip; 1919–1990
Johnson, William H. (Bill, Wise, Big C); 1895–1988
Spearman, Frederick D. (Babe); 1917–2010

Cypress Hills National Cemetery, Brooklyn, NY
Douglass, Edward (Eddie); 1887–1936
Hudspeth, Robert (Highpocket); 1894–1935
Mongin, Samuel (Sam, Polly); 1884–1936
Noble, Rafael Miguel (Ray, Sam); 1919–1998
Robinson, Jack Roosevelt (Jackie); 1919–1972

Evergreen Cemetery, Brooklyn, NY
Garcia, John Juan; 1876–1904
King, William (Dolly); 1916–1969
Robinson, Luther (Bill, Bojangles); 1878–1949

Ferncliff Cemetery, Hartsdale, NY
Stanley, John Wesley (Neck); 1905–1958

Forest Lawn Cemetery & Gardens, Buffalo, NY
Hardy, Arthur Wesley (Art); 1891–1980
Lockhart, Adolphus J. (A. J., Duke, Arthur); 1901–1993

Frederick Douglass Memorial Park Cemetery, Staten Island, NY
Bryant, Elias (Country Brown); 1895–1937

White, King Solomon (Sol, King); 1868–1955

Greenwood Cemetery, Brooklyn, NY
McHenry, Henry Lloyd (Cream); 1910–1981
Strong, Nathaniel C. (Nat); 1874–1935

Long Island National Cemetery, Farmingdale, NY
Brooks, Irvin Woodberry (aka Chester A.); 1891–1966
Buchanan, Chester Floyd (Buck); 1906–1964
Deas, James Alvin (Yank); 1895–1972
Henderson, Curtis Lee (Dan); 1913–1960
Norman, Elbert (Ed, Alton); 1897–1968
Pace, Benjamin H. (Brother); 1894–?
Redding, Richard (Cannonball, Dick); 1893–1948
Semler, James Aloysius (Soldier Boy); 1891–1955
Scott, Robert (Bob); 1892–1949
Starks, Otis (Lefty); 1896–1965

Memory's Garden, Colonie, NY
Mitchell, Arthur Harold; 1914–1994
Walker, Sr., Edsall Elliott (Big, Catskill, Wild Man); 1910–1997

Mount Hope Cemetery, Rochester, NY
King, Leonard D.; 1900–1984

Mount Olivet Cemetery, Maspeth, Queens, NY
Pettus, William Thomas (Zack, Bill); 1884–1924
Wilkins, Barron DeWare; 1865–1924

Mount Olivet Cemetery, Tonawanda, NY
Miro, Pedro; 1918–1996

Oakview Cemetery, Frankfort, NY
Fowler, John W. (Bud); 1858–1913

Oakwood Cemetery, Troy, NY
Harrell, William (Billy); 1928–2014

Park View Cemetery, Schenectady, NY
Ewing, William Monroe (Buck); 1903–1979

Pine Hill Cemetery, Throop, NY
Northrup, John Henry (Harry, Zip); 1882–1944

Pinelawn Cemetery, Farmingdale, NY
Robertson, Peter (Creole Pete); 1905–1980

Saint Raymond Cemetery, Bronx, NY
McMahon, Roderick James (Jess); 1882–1954
Vazquez, Armando Bernando; 1922–2008

Spring Forest Cemetery, Binghamton, NY
Taylor, Robert (Lightning, Flash); 1916–1999

Vale Cemetery, Schenectady, NY
Wickware, Frank Ellis (Red Ant, Big Red, Smiley); 1888–1967

Woodlawn Cemetery, Bronx, NY
Beckwith, Christopher John (Beck); 1900–1956
Connor, John W.; 1876–1926
Pompez, Gonzalo Alejandro (Alex); 1888–1974
Shipp, Jr., Jesse Alright; 1881–1922

Woodlawn Cemetery, Syracuse, NY
Anderson, Andrew W. (Andy); 1902–1989

Index

Numbers in *bold italics* indicate pages with photographs.